The
Suppressed History
OF AMERICA

"Set against the compelling backdrop of Lewis and Clark's historic first crossing of the North American continent, *The Suppressed History of America* breaks new ground and provides interesting food for thought, both for traditional students of American history and for those intrigued by the call of unresolved ancient mysteries."

LAIRD SCRANTON, AUTHOR OF *THE COSMOLOGICAL ORIGINS OF MYTH AND SYMBOL* AND *THE SCIENCE OF THE DOGON*

"*The Suppressed History of America* is a thorough, well-documented, fast-paced exploration of the United States' greatest mystery and adventure—the Lewis and Clark expedition."

ÓCHÁNI LELE, AUTHOR OF *TEACHINGS OF THE SANTERÍA GODS* AND *THE DILOGGÚN*

"*The Suppressed History of America* . . . is a refreshing new addition to the field of the alternative history of the United States. Well researched and written, this book will serve to increase the interest in the full story of the great American explorer Meriwether Lewis. The authors present a cogent argument that Lewis was probably murdered, partly to cover up the profound discoveries he and Clark made in the early nineteenth century."

STEPHEN S. MEHLER, AUTHOR OF *THE LAND OF OSIRIS* AND *FROM LIGHT INTO DARKNESS*

Lewis & Clark Expedition

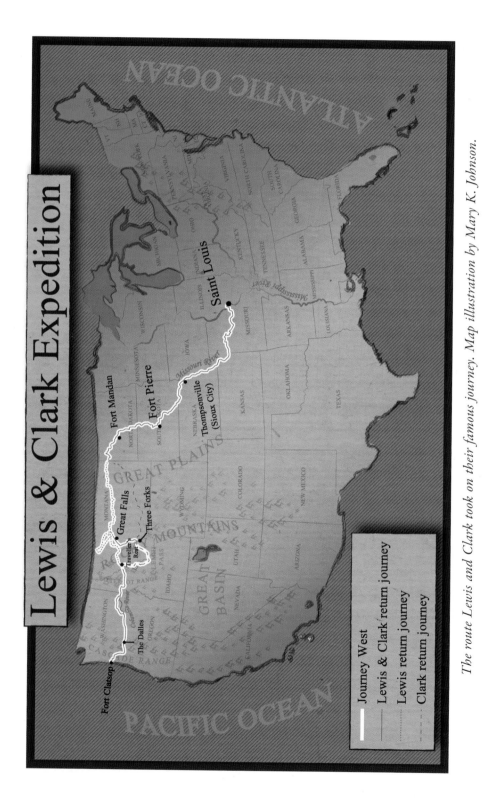

The route Lewis and Clark took on their famous journey. Map illustration by Mary K. Johnson.

The
Suppressed History
of AMERICA

The Murder of Meriwether Lewis and
the Mysterious Discoveries of the
Lewis and Clark Expedition

PAUL SCHRAG and
XAVIANT HAZE

Bear & Company
Rochester, Vermont • Toronto, Canada

Bear & Company
One Park Street
Rochester, Vermont 05767
www.BearandCompanyBooks.com

SUSTAINABLE FORESTRY INITIATIVE Certified Sourcing
www.sfiprogram.org
SFI-00854

Text stock is SFI certified

Bear & Company is a division of Inner Traditions International

Library of Congress Cataloging-in-Publication Data
Schrag, Paul.
  The suppressed history of America : the murder of Meriwether Lewis and the mysterious discoveries of the Lewis and Clark Expedition / Paul Schrag and Xaviant Haze.
      p. cm.
  Includes bibliographical references and index.
  Summary: "An investigation into the discoveries of Lewis and Clark and other early explorers of America and the terrible acts committed to suppress them"— Provided by publisher.
  ISBN 978-1-59143-122-0
  1. Lewis, Meriwether, 1774–1809—Death and burial. 2. Lewis and Clark Expedition (1804–1806) 3. Indians of North America—History. 4. America— Discovery and exploration—Pre-Columbian. I. Haze, Xaviant. II. Title.
  F592.7.L42S34 2011
  970.01—dc22

2011007845

Printed and bound in the United States by Lake Book Manufacturing, Inc. The text stock is SFI certified. The Sustainable Forestry Initiative® program promotes sustainable forest management.

10   9   8   7   6   5

Text design by Jon Desautels and layout by Priscilla Baker
This book was typeset in Garamond Premier Pro with Granjon used as a display typeface

To send correspondence to the authors of this book, mail a first-class letter to the authors c/o Inner Traditions • Bear & Company, One Park Street, Rochester, VT 05767, and we will forward the communication.

Contents

Foreword

If it flies in the face of convention, suppress it. If it contradicts accepted academic dogma, reject it. If it opens minds, condemn it. If it turns history upside down, make sure it never sees the light of day. So has it been down through time. So it was in the late 1800s when Smithsonian executive John Wesley Powell and his colleagues decided that, for humanity's good, they had best systematically destroy the vast amount of accumulated evidence proving that several Native American Indian tribes were most probably descended from ancient European visitors to the New World. Yes, in the minds of duplicitous psychopaths, destruction is always sanctified by some dubious pretext. Nevertheless, regardless of the blitzkrieg on truth, it is always a day for celebration when nefarious plots are foiled or exposed.

Reading through the pages of this book gives me this sense of satisfaction. It also furnishes me with additional proof of the devilry of people in high places. Although I have always been aware of the extraordinary lengths to which brainwashers will go to engender the consensus trance that suits their overall agenda for world control, it is valuable to learn even more about their ruthless and unceasing campaign to mislead us. Page after page, I was left aghast.

Particularly formidable are the revelations concerning the vaunted

Smithsonian Institution that was legally established in 1846. Curiously, its founder, James Smithson (1765–1829), never visited the United States. It is not even clear what motivated him to found the institution. Its facade gives an impression of nobility and academic prowess, and its cathedral-like architecture exudes an aura of established credibility. The average visitor is not inclined to guess that the carefully arranged displays and tour-guide rhetoric are contrived to give them a false impression of America's past. No, they walk away feeling intrigued, informed, and certain. Little do they suspect that they've been royally deceived.

Since its advent, the Smithsonian Institution and its eleven satellite museums have been visited by millions of people from all over the world. It is, according to its own PR spin, dedicated to "the increase and diffusion of knowledge among men." That's nice. But is it true?

Well, no! Unfortunately, as this book reveals, it is not true. Too bad the Smithsonian's founders and board of regents decided to obliterate the evidence that contradicted consensual notions about America's ancient history. Reading of their Machiavellian intrigue compels us to ask, yet again, what our world would be without such egregious censorship. Where would we be if humanity had open access to the information that has been sequestered and hidden away from sight? We can only guess.

These are a few of the questions that have perpetually arisen in my mind as, through the years, I delved into relatively unexplored areas of history. Personally, I have long been interested in ancient origins. My father enjoyed taking my brother and me to many megalithic sites in Northern Ireland. He did not have the same interest in them as I later developed, but in his own casual way he marveled at the stone circles and passage graves and made us aware of their mysterious history. That might have been the beginning for me.

Later, in the mid-1980s, I decided to revisit several sites to take measurements and photographs. I wanted to make a more precise study of Newgrange, Knowth, Dowth, Tara, Navan, Cong, Grianan de Aileach, Dun Aonghasa, and other extraordinary places. Of course, it wasn't long before I realized that what Irish people generally knew about their ancient forebears was largely nonsense.

There was much more to what I was seeing, and I was determined to find out why these places existed, why they turned out to be aligned to the constellations, and why they had been designed so that one site in a field geomantically aligned with every other similar site in the country. I soon discovered that I was not getting my answers from the many contemptuous and myopic tour guides I encountered. It troubled me to think that the situation was probably not very different in other countries of the world. If what I suspected was true, something had to be done. Well, little did I know it at the time, but my real education had begun.

Fortunately I was never inclined to accept the implausible and often blatantly contrived jive I was taught in school and that I read in most mainstream or officially vetted history books. Whatever I found intriguing about the history of my own land, and other places, was frequently labeled and dismissed as "mythological." It took time for me to realize that this is one of the most misapplied terms in the English language. In my opinion, it is one of many talismanic words used to entrain minds. It induces us to partition time, history, and reality into hemispheres that are then deliberately dislocated, and rarely if ever reunited. I know for a fact that this is what passes for education and intelligence in today's world. One is considered educated as long as one does not question the flagrant trickery and deemed intelligent as long as one continues to practice the same travesty during one's own academic career and intellectual feats.

Yes, declare something a "myth" or "legend," and you can be sure that most people will regard it dismissively. A fact or event so labeled does not have the same impact or significance as that which an average person blithely takes for "reality." Cross that line, break that trance to begin asking troublesome questions, and you risk a lot. Like Meriwether Lewis, the truth seeker might find the journey into the unknown to be a perilous one.

To change your settings and walk the alternative road takes work and time. To think critically and doubt what you are supposed to believe takes guts. To read between the lines and fill in the blanks takes audacity and imagination. To negotiate the labyrinth of age-old deception takes determination, self-assuredness, and passion. Moreover, the reward sought by a legitimate truth-seeker is not that of public adulation but the breaking of a trance, the overcoming of formidable obstacles, the discernment of a subtle but perfidious lie-machinery, the exposure of truth, and the attainment of clear understanding. Once that great gift is won, it is an additional boon to be able to communicate and share one's interests and discoveries with the world at large. This is because there is no end to the chain of revelation. There will never be an end to the journey of discovery and awakening. One find leads to a second; one "Eureka" moment paves the way to another; one person's life struggle gives purpose to another seeker's adventure. What truly bonds one human being to another is not blood but ideas.

We may traverse valleys, mountain ranges, and oceans, as did Meriwether Lewis, or we may negotiate more abstract landscapes—those of heart, mind, and soul. If we study nature we end up finding out more about ourselves. If we study other people—other nations, races, and tribes—we end up knowing a great deal more about our own existence. We also find out how many obstacles stand in the way of our goal. We become familiar with the stench of deception, the shades of falsehood, the hideous complexion of lies. We perfect our ability to discern truth because we become so familiar with its opposite. We come upon the truth because we have become immune to everything that stands in contradistinction to it. Our minds receive the gift of truth once we reject everything that takes its place or attempts to stand in its stead. Genius and enlightenment rise from no other foundation and take seed in no other "soil" than the mind with zero tolerance for the false and contrived.

Sadly, most people don't lose much sleep over the existence of obscene people or institutes hell-bent on keeping secret the facts about our world. Even when most people are told that crimes—such as those revealed in these pages—have occurred, they don't let it get under their skin. They are more likely to retort, So what? What can I do about it? A few old relics went missing. The last surviving member of an ancient and mysterious race finally passed away, taking his knowledge with him. Okay, that's tough. History books give us a deliberately skewed view of the past. A high-placed official's ego got out of control, and he took liberties with valuable data. It happens! He's long dead, so nothing can be done. All too often this is what we get. All too often there is no public uprising, outcry, or demand for restitution.

Having said that, one positive outcome is possible. Regardless of how much time has elapsed, we can at least learn who was who, and who did what. We can learn about past underhanded machinations so that we are less likely to fall for similar antics in our own age. Additionally, the names of great men and women, who in their own time defended the truth and had the good of humanity at heart, can be remembered and honored. In my mind, this is what particularly distinguishes this book.

Of additional interest to me are the author's questions about the origin of various important Native American tribes, such as the deeply spiritual Missouri Mandans (first encountered in 1797), and the even more ancient and mysterious Mound Builders of Ohio. His work makes the reader acutely aware of important problems concerning ancient American history. How did the earliest humans get to the continent of America? Where did they come from? What compelled them to vacate their original habitats? What did the ancients say about their own origins? What are the most important differences between the many Native American tribes?

Why do so many tribes (of both the Southern and the Northern Hemispheres) speak of extraterrestrial visitation, giants, and evil angels whose diabolical behavior compelled the gods to send a cataclysm to wreck the world? Why did certain tribes (Kogi, Iroquois, Cherokee, Hopi, Pueblo, Seneca, Apache, and others) prophesy a coming age of severe moral and spiritual decline?

Why were ancient Chinese coins found in the state of Washington? Did the Ainu people (the prehistoric inhabitants of China) once frequent the northwestern United States? Why is the language of the Mandan people so similar to Gaelic? Why were the garments of Mandan women found to be similar to those of Nordic women? Who built the ziggurats, temples, and precisely positioned sacerdotal cities of Mexico? Who were the Olmecs? Who was the so-called Feathered Serpent, and why was he described as being of pale complexion? On and on go the questions.

Naturally no single book or encyclopedia can ever hope to provide us with complete answers to these kinds of questions. Having said that, the authors of this book have done justice to most of them. They warrant my acknowledgment for even asking questions of this kind and for bravely considering controversial theories in response. This work certainly shows us that currently we do not have all the answers to the many mysteries raised, at least not from official sources. More crucially, in all likelihood, we will never get our answers as long as the present academic status quo remains intact and unchallenged. The findings herein stress that even when solutions are proffered by open-minded and intelligent people, they are all too often shot down in flames. It is quite a challenge to come upon a truth after decades of searching and labor. It is also a challenge to transmit that truth to humanity. The latter struggle often proves more laborious than the former.

I have personally found this to be the case. I too have dealt with similar mysteries and conundrums about America's past in my own book titled *The Irish Origins of Civilization*. In volume one, in the chapter "American Arya," I briefly cover some of the sensational discoveries of Augustus Le Plongeon and Barry Fell. The earthshaking finds of these men clearly show us that ancient Europeans had indeed visited and perhaps even settled in the Americas. Furthermore, in my "Irish Origins" and "Atlantis" volumes I referred to a book titled *Fair Gods and Stone Faces* by Constance Irwin that I have kept in my possession since the 1980s. The author of this hard-to-find masterpiece provides ample evidence of the presence of white people in South America, people regarded by Toltec, Maya, and Inca sages as the bringers of civilization. And like those southern tribes, the Mandans, Zuni, Hopi, and other pre-Columbian tribes of North America also spoke of a worldwide cataclysm that drove their terrified ancestors under ground.

Before that time, before the antediluvian world was destroyed, the nations and races were constellated. They lived together, without division, on a great continent in the Atlantic region. It was from this ancient land, say the legends, that the godlike people came, the land of Pahána—or "lost white brother." Are we to disregard these accounts as yet more "myths"? Are we to pretend that the Olmec stone heads and vast megalithic ruins of Easter Island, Chaco Canyon, Palenque, Cuzco, and the Bolivian Andes (not to mention those in Ireland, northern India, and Egypt) are merely figments of our imagination?

As to this book's main theme, we can be fairly certain that Meriwether Lewis was murdered. Personally, I suspect Thomas Jefferson and his crew, but if Aaron Burr and his gang turn out to be the culprits it won't surprise me in the least. Each reader must come to his or her own conclusions on the controversy. In any case, I can assure the reader that the names "Lewis and Clark" elicited no glazed expressions when I was in school. In my day, every school kid in England and Ireland knew their names. The eyes of most boys and girls lit up once they were mentioned, and we listened with fascination when our history or geography teachers recounted the story of their harrowing adventures and exploits. Their grueling traversals and terrifying encounters thrilled us long before the advent of Hollywood's make-believe Indiana Jones, that's for sure. Therefore, it is with pride that I write this foreword for this fine book. Not only was I eager to discover the truth about Meriwether Lewis's life and death, but I also consider it a duty to assist in the restoration of the governor's good name and reputation. It is a noble thing to honor great men and women of the past, particularly those whose contributions have either been forgotten or deliberately downplayed by humanity's scurrilous Machiavellian misleaders.

Governor Lewis apparently suffered the same fate as many other ardent souls who labored to discover the truth about humankind's origins. He went the way of Wilhelm Reich, who discovered the secrets of the spirit-body connection; and of Raymond Royal Rife, who discovered how to obliterate cancerous disease.

Meriwether Lewis's discoveries suffered the same fate as those of Augustus Le Plongeon, Gerald Massey, Reverend Robert Taylor, E. A. Wallis Budge, Immanuel Velikovsky, L. A. Waddell, Comyns Beaumont, Barry Fell, Professor Thomas L. Thompson, and so many other geniuses and pioneers I could mention. The tribulations of these men must be reviewed. Injustices against their names and reputations must be set aright. It is a lofty undertaking that must be made with courage and indefatigable passion. The great work of exploration and restoration continues. Truth Against the World!

MICHAEL TSARION

Born in Northern Ireland, Michael Tsarion is an expert on the occult histories of Ireland and America. He has made the deepest researches into Atlantis, the origins of evil, and the Irish origins of civilization. He is author of *Atlantis, Alien Visitation and Genetic Manipulation*; *Astro-Theology and Sidereal Mythology*; and *The Irish Origins of Civilization*. He has had numerous radio and television appearances, including the Syfy channel's documentary *Quest for Atlantis*.

Introduction

Some of the most crucial tales of American history are contained in the journals of Meriwether Lewis, explorer, historian, scientist, and soldier. But behind the tales of frontier bluster and adventure are stories that are far more fascinating. These tales have haunted academics and historians for decades—stories of lost cultures, strange monoliths, anachronistic artifacts, and enigmatic races found in the shadows and cracks between America's official versions of history. The death of Meriwether Lewis, his exploration of the American wilderness, and many of the discoveries that lie along his path are steeped in mystery.

The contention that Lewis was murdered is not a new one. Rumors about murder began circulating as soon as news of his death emerged.

Historical accounts, letters, and newspaper reports compiled by biographers such as Stephen Ambrose and Richard Dillon suggest that the people who knew Lewis were initially shocked, saddened, and confused about the circumstances surrounding his death.

Lewis was respected by all who knew him as a fearless, quick-witted adventurer of powerful constitution and indefatigable will. When asked why he chose Lewis over a scientist or researcher to catalog the adventure west, then president Thomas Jefferson said, "It was impossible to find a character who to compleat science in botany, natural history, mineralogy & astronomy, joined the firmness and constitution &

1

character, prudence, habits adapted to the woods & familiarity with the Indian manners & character requisite for this undertaking. All the latter qualifications Capt. Lewis has."[1]

The same qualities that made Lewis the president's first choice to lead the expedition west—strength, savvy, fearlessness, strength of character, education, and military wit—are the same qualities that cast doubt on reports of his deterioration and suicide. They're also the same qualities that likely got him killed. In chapter 10 we explore the politics of Lewis's day and why certain factions may have wanted him out of the way.

With regard to Lewis's actual death, there were no eyewitnesses, and there is a list of strange circumstances that remain unaddressed and unanswered by official accounts of his alleged suicide. How did an expert marksman manage to shoot himself so ineffectively, languishing for hours, then finally manage to cut himself with razors from head to toe to finish the job? The answer, it seems, should be simple. The once-great wilderness explorer turned political powerhouse was murdered.

But history is never that simple, and the truth of history is notoriously difficult to pin down. Many historians, who have become lost in a sort of wilderness of their own, still believe in history as written and feel content to piece it together from the writings and research of other academics. They offer dry, lifeless regurgitations—fallow truths uttered from deep-red high-backed leather chairs, resting by a fire in New England. They are content with history as long as it is deemed academically sound and safe.

This book is not a safe journey. This is an invitation to return to the wilderness, where history is pieced together from bits of exploration, strange and wonderful experience, passion, and poetry. The place where these topics coalesce—pre-Columbian America and the exploration of Lewis and Clark—has been danced around for years. Much of the story has simply been brushed aside as mere speculation or fictitious legend.

Despite persistent criticism and opposition from official circles, a different picture of early America has begun to emerge. It is one that requires a different approach to the way we catalog history . . .

One

The Olmec Riddles

The murder of Meriwether Lewis marked the inception of an academic war over how to define the America that existed before the Spanish conquistadores, French explorers, and British adventurers arrived in the so-called New World. This intellectual battle has been waged for centuries now by two factions of scholars—the diffusionists and the independent inventionists.

To this day the diffusionists are spoken of with derision in mainstream academic circles, as they dig into the past with the same courage that characterized Lewis and his journey west. Like Lewis, these rogue scholars continue to unearth evidence that America was visited long before Columbus by explorers crossing both the Pacific and Atlantic Oceans. Moreover, these scholars continue to unearth evidence of rich, vibrant, highly evolved cultures that existed in ancient America. This growing volume of archaeological evidence stands in clear contradiction to many key assumptions held by America's founders and their scholarly counterparts, the so-called independent inventionists.

The inventionist perspective remains the standard among archaeologists and suggests that natives of the American continent are descended from Ice Age relatives who crossed the Bering Strait and developed in complete isolation—until, that is, they were "discovered" by Spanish, French, and British explorers during the late fifteenth century. In the early days of America it was the federal government and its proponents who were most interested in characterizing the continent as an untrammeled paradise populated by savages.

This set of assumptions gave early explorers and exploiters of the American continent the justification they needed to co-opt and pillage its resources, wage war on its native people, and occupy its lands with impunity. It was the perspective that America's government officials held as they tamed America's terrain and battled its people for control of the vast stores of resources that would fuel the creation of their New World. It also became the perspective that was later adopted by the Smithsonian Institution, which, more than any other organization, has defined our understanding of America's origins. Since its inception in the 1800s, the Smithsonian joined the powers in Washington in vigorously promoting the idea that America was an untouched landscape before Europeans arrived to "claim" it. Simply put, the Smithsonian's initial administrators followed the direction already chosen by America's early leaders, supported by their own inherited cultural and scholarly myopia.

Paradoxically enough, however, it was an agent of the Smithsonian Institution, Matthew Sterling, who championed one of the first contentious examples of cultural diffusionism when he began investigations into the mysterious Olmecs and the origins of Mayan culture in what are now the southern reaches of Mexico.

The Olmecs are considered by some historians to be the mother culture to the Mayan, Aztec, and Inca tribes. A pre-Columbian people, they inhabited the lowlands of south-central Mexico, in a region now occupied by the states of Veracruz and Tabasco. The Olmec were prominent from 1200 BCE to about 400 BCE, according to various accounts. They were the first Mesoamerican civilization and planted seeds of other civilizations throughout the region. The Olmecs are credited with being the first Mesoamerican culture to practice ritual blood sacrifice and play the Mesoamerican ballgame—practices that became the hallmarks of several subsequent tribes and civilizations.

From the steamy jungles of Mexico's southern Gulf Coast to the modern countries of Guatemala, Honduras, Belize, Costa Rica, and El

Salvador, the Olmecs built large settlements, established trade routes, and developed religious iconography and rituals.

The rise of the Olmec civilization was driven largely by the region's ecology, which included well-watered alluvial soil and a network of rivers that provided the Olmecs with a useful transportation system. The region where Olmec culture took root is similar to other cultural spawning grounds such as the Nile, Indus, and Yellow River Valleys. This rich environment fostered a dense population and the rise of an elite culture that exploited the region's stores of obsidian and jade, for example, to create works of art that have defined the Olmec culture. Exploration of this culture was sparked by artifacts circulating through the pre-Columbian art market in the late nineteenth and early twentieth centuries. To this day, Olmec artwork is considered among ancient America's most marvelous achievements.

Archaeologists consider San Lorenzo the earliest of the major Olmec ceremonial centers. Located in the open country around the Rio Chiquito in southern Veracruz, it rested on a massive, sculpted salt plateau, with a series of manmade ravines constructed on three of its four sides. This structure represents the earliest ball court in Mesoamerica, complete with a system of carved stone drains.

Richard Diehl, professor of anthropology at the University of Alabama, has conducted archaeological investigations all over Mexico and authored the essential guide on the Olmecs. Diehl echoes Ann Cyphers, an Olmec scholar at Mexico's National Autonomous University, when he explains, "San Lorenzo shows clear evidence of class structure," and "there were probably a number of different populations, forming groups that rose and fell over time and shifted alliances. I don't think there was any political integration."[1]

And while Diehl offers admiration for their drains and class structure, he makes very little mention of the Olmecs' dramatic end, which has been explained away by theories of an internal uprising, ecological disaster, or hostile invasion. When San Lorenzo was discovered, almost all its large sculptures were defaced, buried, or destroyed. Like

Meriwether Lewis, the Olmec people met a mysterious end that has yet to be satisfactorily explained.

Some of the carved works at San Lorenzo include the legendary massive Olmec head sculptures, which weigh as many as forty tons and stand nearly three meters high. These massive heads have vexed archaeologists since their discovery, showing characteristics that have led many to assert that they are African in origin or were created by people of African descent.

First discovered by plantation workers, the colossal sculptures were reported in the 1869 *Bulletin of the Mexican Geographical and Statistical Society* as "a magnificent sculpture that most amazingly represents an Ethiopian." The report included a drawing clearly outlining the stone heads' African features. What appears to be a bit of honest investigative reporting was too controversial to be taken seriously at the time, and the idea of Africans residing in Mexico was quickly and largely forgotten.

Decades later Smithsonian curator Matthew Sterling, fascinated by dusty tomes pulled from the basements of the museum, began a personal exploration into the history of the Olmecs. At the time, Sterling's findings were considered blasphemous by an academic community dedicated to the study of Mayan culture. Until Sterling's investigations in the late 1930s and early '40s, Mayan culture was considered the seed of all culture in Mesoamerica. Work by archaeologists such as Phillip Drucker and Robert Hetzer, who used modern methods such as carbon dating to determine the age of Olmec artifacts, later vindicated Sterling and his views. Though not widely acknowledged, Sterling's discoveries, publications, and perseverance in defending them would undermine a position long held by his own organization, the Smithsonian Institution. Kathy O'Halleran, author of *Indigenous People's History,* says:

> The outcome of the Olmec-Maya controversy is noted in the intellectual community as a shining example of the need for open minds. Above all, it shows how major new archaeological discoveries can be made even in the mid-twentieth century and how the intellectual

perseverance of a minority viewpoint in the archaeological community can lead to eventual acceptance—even after initial rejection.[2]

After years of research, in 1938 Sterling traveled to the southwestern Mexican lowland, armed with well-prepared journals and funds from the National Geographic Society. His goal was simple: uncover the seeming mystery of a discarded ancient people.

Sterling's first stop was Tres Zapotes, an ancient Olmec city on the western edge of the Los Tuxtlas Mountains. Tres Zapotes is best known for its impressive garden of carved steles, altars, and colossal stone heads, all of which were discovered at least a hundred miles away from the nearest source of the stone from which they were carved.

Among the monuments at Tres Zapotes was Stele C, a freestanding stone monument carved from basalt. The stele is engraved with an undecipherable script, which surrounds a jaguar sitting on a throne. On the opposite side of the stele is the second-oldest Mesoamerican long-count calendar date ever to have been unearthed. The calendar is a nonrepeating vigesimal (based on factors of twenty) numeral system; it was apparently used by several Mesoamerican cultures, most notably the Mayans.

Sterling also discovered an imposing fourteen-foot-high stele with carvings that showed an encounter between two tall men, both dressed in elaborate robes and wearing elegant shoes with turned-up toes. Erosion or deliberate mutilation had defaced one of the figures. The other was intact. It so obviously depicted a Caucasian male with a high-bridged nose and a long, flowing beard that the bemused archaeologists christened it "Uncle Sam." These monuments, whether they resembled bearded Caucasians or African kings, have amazed and bewildered experts and the layperson for generations.

Author Graham Hancock, an acclaimed alternative historian intrigued by the anomalies associated with the Olmecs, traveled to the ruins at La Venta, a civic and ceremonial center and home to one of the oldest pyramids in Mesoamerica. Hancock, dumbfounded at the immense complexity of the structures, writes:

In the centre of the park, like some magic talisman, stood an enormous grey boulder, almost ten feet tall, carved in the shape of a helmeted African head. Here, then, was the first mystery of the Olmecs, a monumental piece of sculpture, more than 2000 years old. It was unmistakably the head of an African man wearing a close-fitting helmet with long chinstraps. Plugs pierced the lobes of the ears, and the entire face was concentrated above thick, down-curving lips. It would be impossible for a sculptor to invent all the different combined characteristics of an authentic racial type. The portrayal of an authentic combination of racial characteristics therefore implied strongly a human model had been used. I walked around the great head a couple of times. It was 22 feet in circumference, weighed 19.8 tons, stood almost 8 feet high, had been carved out of solid basalt, and displayed clearly an authentic combination of racial characteristics. My own view is that the Olmec heads present us with physiologically accurate images of real individuals. Charismatic and powerful African men whose presence in Central America 3000 years ago has not yet been explained by scholars.[3]

Hancock personally studied the same stele that Sterling had sixty years earlier. Two things seemed very clear to him:

The encounter scene it portrayed must, for some reason, have been of immense importance to the Olmecs, hence the grandeur of the stele itself, and the construction of the remarkable stockade of columns built to contain it. And, as was the case with the African heads, it was obvious that the face of the bearded Caucasian man could only have been sculpted from a human model. One was carved in low relief on a heavy and roughly circular slab of stone about three feet in diameter. Dressed in what looked like tight-fitting leggings, his features were those of an Anglo-Saxon. He had a full pointed beard and wore a curious floppy cap on his head. Around his slim waist was tied a flamboyant sash.[4]

These Caucasian figures carved in the stones were uncovered from exactly the same strata as the huge Olmec heads. The La Venta figures and their attire resembled reliefs in Abydos, Egypt, that depict the Battle of Kadesh. Hittite charioteers shown in the reliefs all have long, elaborate robes and shoes with turned-up toes.

Hancock suggests, "It is by no means impossible that these great works preserve the images of peoples from a vanished civilization which embraced several ethnic groups. Strangely, despite the best efforts of archaeologists, not a single, solitary sign of anything that could be described as the 'developmental phase' of Olmec society has been unearthed anywhere in Mexico. These amazing artists appeared to have come from nowhere."[5]

Evidence suggests that rather than developing slowly, the Olmec civilization emerged all at once and fully formed. The transition period from primitive to advanced society appears to have been so short that it baffles modern anthropologists, archaeologists, and historians. Technical skills that should have taken hundreds or even thousands of years to evolve were brought into use almost overnight and with no apparent antecedents whatsoever.

A vivid picture of the end of the Olmec civilization is found in the ancient city of Monte Alban. The city stands on a vast, artificially flattened hilltop overlooking Oaxaca and consists of a huge rectangular area enclosed by groups of pyramids and other buildings that are laid out in precise geometrical relationships to one another.

Hancock visited this site and recorded his discoveries.

I made my way first to the extreme south-west corner of the Monte Alban site. There, stacked loosely against the side of a low pyramid, were the objects I had come all this way to see: several dozen engraved Stele depicting Africans and Caucasians . . . equal in life . . . equal in death. At Monte Alban, however, there seemed to be carved in stone a record of the downfall of these masterful men. It did not look as if this could have been the work of the same people who made the

La Venta sculptures. The standard of craftsmanship was far too low for that. Whoever they were, these artists had attempted to portray the same subjects I had seen at La Venta. There the sculptures had reflected strength, power and vitality. Here, at Monte Alban, the remarkable strangers were corpses. All were naked, most were castrated, and some were curled up in fetal positions as though to avoid showers of blows, others lay sprawled.[6]

At an annual conference of the Institute for the Study of American Cultures, Mike Xu, a professor of modern languages and literature at Texas Christian University, suggests the possibility of direct Chinese influence on the Olmec:

Carved stone blades found in Guatemala, dating from approximately 1100 B.C., are distinctly Chinese in pattern, and share uncanny resemblances to glyphs from the Shang Dynasty. The problem is not whether Asians reached Mesoamerica before Columbus. The problem is when did they arrive, and what did they do here? Any proposal that smacks of diffusionism in today's academic climate is immediately dismissed as irresponsible at best, malevolent at worst. Here are all these American scholars, speaking European languages, and they dare to say no, there was never any diffusion; and yes, all Western Hemisphere cultures are indigenous![7]

In his most recent work, *The Olmecs: America's First Civilization,* Richard Diehl wrote more than 200 pages but spent only a brief part of the discussion on the subject of diffusionism.

The origins of Olmec culture have intrigued scholars and lay people alike since Tres Zapotes Colossal Head I, a gigantic stone human head with African features, discovered in Veracruz 140 years ago. Since that time, Olmec culture and art have been attributed to seafaring Africans, Egyptians, Nubians, Phoenicians, Atlanteans,

Japanese, Chinese, and other ancient wanderers. As often happens, the truth is infinitely more logical, if less romantic: the Olmecs were Native Americans who created a unique culture in southeastern Mexico's Isthmus of Tehuantepec.

Archaeologists now trace Olmec origins back to pre-Olmec cultures in the region and there is no credible evidence for major intrusions from the outside. Furthermore, not a single bona fide artifact of old world origin has ever appeared in an Olmec archaeological site, or for that matter anywhere else in Mesoamerica.[8]

With this entry, Diehl swiftly dismisses all theories and evidence of transoceanic contact. It is important to note how difficult it is to determine what a bona fide old-world artifact would be, since old-world and new-world articles are often indistinguishable. Also, Diehl offers no further information on the cultures from which the Olmecs are presumably derived. For the Olmecs to actually be Africans—not just look like them—they would almost certainly have come to the Isthmus of Tehuantepec via ship. But such voyages are dismissed immediately by most scholars, and the Olmecs have simply been characterized as local boys.

While excavating in the Mexican state of Veracruz in 2006, archaeologist Maria del Carmen Rodriguez discovered a stone slab with 3,000-year-old writing previously unknown to scholars. The slab was covered in carved symbols that appeared to be those of a complex writing system, of which she writes:

> Finding a heretofore unknown writing system is rare. One of the last major ones to come to light, scholars say, was the Indus Valley script, recognized from excavations in 1924. Now, scholars are tantalized by a message in stone in a script unlike any other and a text they cannot read. They are excited by the prospect of finding more of this writing, and eventually deciphering it, to crack open a window on one of the most enigmatic ancient civilizations. The inscription on the Mexican stone, with 28 distinct signs, some of which are

repeated, for a total of 62, has been tentatively dated from at least 900 B.C., possibly earlier. That is 400 or more years before writing was known to have existed in Mesoamerica, the region from central Mexico through much of Central America, and by extension, anywhere in the hemisphere. Previously, no script had been associated unambiguously with the Olmec culture, which flourished along the Gulf of Mexico in Veracruz and Tabasco well before the Zapotec and Maya people rose to prominence elsewhere in the region. Until now, the Olmec were known mainly for the colossal stone heads they sculptured and displayed at monumental buildings in their ruling cities.[9]

Several paired sequences of signs have prompted speculation that the text may contain couplets of poetry.

Experts who have examined the symbols on the stone slab said they would need many more examples before they could hope to decipher and read what is written. It appeared, they said, that the symbols in the inscription were unrelated to later Mesoamerican scripts, suggesting that this Olmec writing might have been practiced for only a few generations and may never have spread to surrounding cultures.

Beyond advanced linguistic and literary systems, the Olmecs also seemed to have possessed advanced knowledge of mathematics and navigation.

Astronaut Gordon Cooper became interested in the Olmecs during his final years with NASA. During a treasure-hunting expedition in Mexico, he encountered Olmec ruins, which led to a startling discovery.

One day, accompanied by a *National Geographic* photographer, we landed in a small plane on an island in the Gulf of Mexico. Local residents pointed out to us pyramid-shaped mounds, where we found ruins, artifacts and bones. On the examinations back in Texas, the artifacts were determined to be 5,000 years old. When we learned of the age of the artifacts we realized that what we'd found had nothing to do with seventeenth-century Spain. . . . I contacted the Mexican government and was put in touch with the head of the national archaeology department, Pablo Bush Romero.[10]

Together with Mexican archaeologists, the two returned to the site. After some excavating, Cooper writes,

The age of the ruins was confirmed: 3000 B.C. Compared with other advanced civilizations, relatively little was known about the Olmec. Engineers, farmers, artisans, and traders, the Olmecs had a remarkable civilization. But it is still not known where they originated. . . . Among the findings that intrigued me most were celestial navigation symbols and formulas that, when translated, turned out to be mathematical formulas used to this day for navigation, and accurate drawings of constellations, some of which would not be officially "discovered" until the age of modern telescopes. Why have celestial navigation signs if they weren't navigating celestially?

And he asks: "If someone had helped the Olmecs with this knowledge, from whom did they get it?"[11]

The enigmas left behind by the Olmecs are staggering. In stark contrast to nearly every assumption held about pre-Columbian cultures, much evidence suggests that people from distant civilizations arrived on the continents "discovered" by explorers such as Lewis centuries before.

Can a similar influence be found in North America? And if so, did it still exist during the journey made by Lewis and Clark?

Two

Florida and the Fountain of Youth

Meriwether Lewis wasn't the first intrepid adventurer to suffer a dark fate while discovering secrets on the American continent. In 1508, sixteen years after Columbus's first voyage, Juan Ponce de Leon discovered gold on the island of Puerto Rico. Within a short span of time, the people of the island paradise were extinct. Many died in battle defending their homeland. Others succumbed to diseases incurred during their enslavement by foreign invaders who came to exploit rich stores of gold ore and other precious resources. Like Lewis, his discoveries made Ponce de Leon an instant celebrity and one of the richest men in the New World.

Boasting a slightly less glorious early career than Lewis, de Leon had begun his naval career as a pirate for hire, attacking ships belonging to the Moors. This experience earned him a chance to undertake a journey to the Americas at the same time that Christopher Columbus was making his second trip to the Americas, to the West Indies, as part of a costly excursion financed by the king and queen of Spain. De Leon sailed from the port of Cadiz and arrived on a Caribbean island dubbed Hispaniola, composing the island that is now host to the Dominican Republic and Haiti, to begin his own series of explorations.

Like Lewis, de Leon was a fearless adventurer who reveled in the chance to serve his superiors by exploring the American continent in search of riches. His arrival at Hispaniola marks the explorer's first connection with the region alleged to host the fountain of youth. Was it here that de Leon first heard of the fabled well? Or had he already been exposed to this legend during his days of looting Moorish ships?

Today, preserved in Aljamiado, is the oldest known story that mentions the mythical fountain. It is a poem written by the Muslims in an encoded language. The poem is called "Al-Iskandur Dhug al Quarnain" and means "Alexander the Two Horned" in Arabic. It tells the story of Alexander the Great going to the land of darkness to find a fountain of youth. It is possible, and some have speculated, that de Leon was aware of these tales via his exploration of Moorish and Muslim customs. The fountain was also mentioned as part of the "Apocryphal Letter of Prester John" that appeared in 1165 in Europe. Three hundred years later, in a world unlike anything they could have imagined, the Spanish explorers may have been enticed by similar legends told by island natives. The exuberance enjoyed after the discovery of new lands could have easily encouraged de Leon to believe that if anyone could find this legendary fountain, he could.

After drifting past the Bahamas and the Florida Keys, de Leon made landfall on the North American mainland, which he mistook initially for an island. Thinking he was still in the Caribbean, de Leon dropped anchor and went ashore somewhere north of what would become the city of St. Augustine.

In 1514 de Leon returned to Spain to report his findings. The fountain of youth was somewhere in those lush isles, he asserted, and the king and queen were convinced that de Leon could find it. On his next excursion de Leon sailed with two hundred men and enough supplies to establish a colony. He landed on the west coast of Florida near what would become Charlotte Harbor and was attacked by Calusa natives. A poisonous arrow wounded de Leon, and most of the Spanish soldiers and colonists were killed. Like Lewis, de Leon's appetite for adventure and exploration led to his untimely death. The few survivors of the skirmish at Charlotte Harbor retreated to Cuba, where de Leon died from his wounds a month later.

Coincidentally, in his initial discovery and in his last battle, de Leon had crept within a short distance of lush areas of deep freshwater sources in Florida; one is near the city of St. Augustine and another in Zephyrhills. The site of his last battle with the natives was a short distance away from the Warm Mineral Springs of North Port, Florida. These massive springs run two thousand feet deep.

Despite the gruesome scuffle and the death of de Leon, the search for the fountain continued. The Spanish conqueror and explorer Pánfilo de Nárvaez (1478–1528) attempted an expedition from Cuba but was caught in a hurricane. The fleet of ships was destroyed, and the survivors washed ashore near modern-day Tampa Bay. Only a man by the name of Cabeza de Vaca and thirty companions survived. Their intention was to reach a Spanish settlement in Mexico and regroup there, but after a battle with hostile natives they rafted their way into southwestern Texas. Traveling west along the Colorado River, de Vaca and the survivors of the ill-fated expedition became the first Europeans to see a bison, or American buffalo. De Vaca returned to Spain nine years later and published his story. It was the bestseller of its time.

In it there are references to encounters with giants, which coincidentally was a recurring theme in Native American folklore. De Vaca's astounding tales mention an encounter during a raid.

When we attempted to cross the large lake, we came under heavy attack from many giant Indians concealed behind trees. Some of our men were wounded in this conflict for which the good armor they wore did not avail. The Indians we had so far seen are all archers. They go naked, are large of body, and appear at a distance like giants. They are of admirable proportions, very spare and of great activity and strength. The bows they use are as thick as the arm, of eleven or twelve palms in length, which they discharge at two hundred paces with so great precision that they miss nothing.[1]

In 1539 Hernando De Soto sailed nine ships into Tampa Bay. As they ventured inland, they encountered the friendly Timucuans. It was customary for the explorers to ensure their safety by holding captive the tribal chiefs. This was done diplomatically, as an invitation. After some reluctance the chiefs agreed to become De Soto's "guests."

When the natives realized becoming guests meant being turned in to slaves, the local tribes, led by Chief Copafi of the Apalachee, sparked an uprising. After weeks of warfare the chief was finally captured in a battle near what would become Tallahassee. He was described as a man of monstrous proportions.

Some of these legends of giants and the search for the fountain of youth are being cast in new light thanks to the work of researcher Duane K. McCullough. McCullough has found different rock islands within Key Largo that contain springs that are unique in composition, thanks to exposure to abundant amounts of nutritious sea salts. These concentrations are attributed to tidal pressure and seasonal freshwater flushing from the Everglades, collecting and mixing within the aquatic pathways that run through cracks in the coral bedrock of the upper Florida Keys. McCullough's research suggests that these rare sea salts contained traces of gold, which is generally greatly diluted in seawater.

Because gold could have been concentrated as a salt by the evaporation of seawater in nearby Florida Bay, and further collected as a heavy metal at the bottom of other basinlike lagoons, it could have been mixed into the local springwaters of the area. This discovery, together with a new understanding of the health benefits of dietary gold salts and how they can improve cell memory, sheds new light on the old legend of waters that impart immortality.

Nutritious salts are common in almost all briny lagoons in the Caribbean. Sulfur, when bonded to a metallic element, creates salts such as calcium sulfate, sodium sulfate, and potassium sulfate, which are essential tissue salts found in any healthy body. Science has discovered that tissue salts and several other important salt compounds are useful in maintaining proper health. If they are not supplied as part of our daily diet, the process of aging accelerates.

These elements do not oxidize at all, and when concentrated by the unique evaporation and flushing process of Florida Bay, they create a golden elixir that can neutralize the aging process if assimilated properly. Research by McCullough and others has helped revive a new interest in the fountain of youth. Some historians speculate that early Spanish explorers may have been close to discovering these wondrous waters, missing them in some instances only by miles.

American magician David Copperfield claimed he had discovered a true fountain of youth amid a cluster of four small islands in the Exuma chain of the Bahamas. He purchased these islands for $50 million in 2006.

"I've discovered a true phenomenon," he told Reuters in a telephone interview. "You can take dead leaves, they come in contact with the water, and become full of life again. Bugs or insects that are near death come in contact with the water, they'll fly away. It's an amazing thing, very, very exciting."[2] Copperfield, who is now fifty-two, says that he hired scientists to conduct an examination of the mystical water, but no further information has been offered.

Property developer Michael Baumann purchased an apartment complex in downtown Miami for $8.5 million in 1998. He planned to build a luxury condominium in its place. After tearing down the older apartments on the property, he was obliged to commission a routine archaeological survey of the site. Bob Carr of the Miami-Dade Historic Preservation Division was called in to conduct the excavation. They discovered holes that had been cut into the limestone bedrock.

Surveyor Ted Riggs, upon examining the layout of these holes, theorized they were part of a circle thirty-eight feet in diameter. Excavation of the path he laid out revealed that there were indeed twenty-four holes forming a perfect circle in the limestone. Examination of earth removed from the site led to the discovery of an array of artifacts, ranging from shell tools and stone ax heads to human teeth and charcoal from fires.

The Miami Circle represents the only evidence of a prehistoric permanent structure cut into the bedrock of the United States.

Signs of an ancient civilization in the Americas predating Columbus's era and the native tribes are abundant, even if they are catalogued incorrectly or ignored. Ponce de Leon, Cabeza de Vaca, and Hernando De Soto, whether looking for the fountain of youth or mapping the state of Florida believing it to be an island, opened the door to further exploration. That exploration unearthed the remains of a city and an earthwork complex dubbed Big Mound, which is situated between the Florida Everglades and the Pitney Flatwoods.

Three

The Mysteries of the
Mississippi Mound Builders

Hernando De Soto's encounters with giants continued as he pushed farther inland in 1539. Traveling with more than six hundred men and two hundred horses, he trekked through North Florida, the southern swamps of Georgia, and the landlocked crossroads of western Alabama. Rodrigo Ranjel, De Soto's private secretary, wrote a diary detailing the expedition. The new lands they explored were ruled by the Native American chief Tuscaloosa.

"De Soto and fifteen soldiers entered the village, and as they rode in, they saw Tuscaloosa stationed on a high place, seated on a mat. Around him stood one hundred of his noblemen, all dressed in richly colored sleeveless cloaks and graceful feathers," writes Ranjel of his encounter with the magnificent tribal leader. "Tuscaloosa appeared to be about forty years old. He appeared to be a giant, or rather was one, and his limbs and face were in proportion to the height of his body. He was handsome, but wore a look of ferocity and grandeur of spirit. He was the tallest and most handsomely shaped Indian that they saw during all their travels."

The diary, first published in 1547, gives a concise account of failed peaceful negotiations and subsequent mayhem.

"As the cavaliers and officers of the camp who preceded De Soto rode forward and arranged themselves in his presence, Tuscaloosa took not the slightest notice of them. He made no move to rise even when De Soto approached." Ranjel tells us that Tuscaloosa was seated on top of a mound at one end of the square, like that of a king. "After a few days of talking and watching colorful war dances, Tuscaloosa joined De Soto on their quest towards Mobile. While on the trail two soldiers turned up missing. When De Soto questioned Tuscaloosa about their whereabouts, he replied that they were not the white men's keepers."[1]

Ranjel then describes the Spaniards' approach toward Mobile. The scouts rode out to De Soto and warned that many Native Americans had gathered for rebellion. De Soto, brave and defiant, approached the town and its high walls. A welcoming committee of painted warriors, clad in robes of skins and headpieces with vibrantly colored feathers, came out to greet them. A group of young Native American maidens followed, dancing and singing to music played on crude instruments.

De Soto entered the town with his most trusted soldiers, Tuscaloosa, and the chief's entourage. The Spaniards stood in a piazza, surrounded by a stream of foreign colors and fluttering sounds. From here De Soto saw some eighty houses within the village. Several of them were described as large enough to hold at least one thousand people. Unknown to De Soto, more than two thousand Native American warriors stood in concealment behind the walls. After some of the chiefs from the town joined him, Tuscaloosa withdrew into the village, warning De Soto with a severe look to leave at once.

Under a hail of arrows, De Soto and most of his men retreated from the village. After regrouping and devising their strategy, the Spaniards gained entry to the village, set fire to the buildings, and massacred the city's inhabitants.

Despite the death and devastation, Tuscaloosa escaped. Riding deep into unknown lands, De Soto and his men marched to capture him. The giant chief disappeared, and the pursuing Spaniards found only abandoned cities with massive mounds. These staggering mounds remain standing throughout the South, especially in the Mississippi Valley.

Professor Robert Silverberg, who has written extensively about Native American history, says:

> The Mississippi mound builders seemed to already have been declining when the Spaniards came around. The Native Americans of the Southeast slid into a less ambitious way of life. Huge mounds were no longer built, around the old mounds the familiar festivals and rituals continued, but hollowly, until their meaning was forgotten and the villagers no longer knew that it was their own great-great-grandfathers who had built the mounds. All of the Native Americans of the Temple Mound regions had only faint and foggy notions of their own history.[2]

Silverberg suggested that the mounds stretched so far back into antiquity that they were not built by Native Americans.

From Oklahoma to northern Georgia, explorations of these mounds have unearthed a variety of items, ranging from simple shells, ceramics, and pipestones to extravagant ceremonial copper axes. Hundreds or perhaps thousands of mounds were built in the Mississippi Delta. Radiocarbon dating has shown that the decline in the Mound Builders population began more than a century before Europeans arrived in the region. The decline and desertion of these people is still a mystery.

During the time of the conquistadors, there was only one group of southeastern Native Americans who appeared to be able to trace their heritage back far enough to include the Mound Builders. These people were the Natchez, who, along with the Choctaw and Chickasaw tribes, were the primary travelers of the natural trail—which they shared with migrating bison, deer, and other animals—that later became the route that Lewis and Clark made famous. Their empire stretched from the delta to the swamps of Louisiana. It's a stretch of land that Meriwether Lewis would become all too familiar with. We know from the writings of French Jesuit Pierre Charlevoix that the Natchez rebelled unsuccessfully against the French in 1729.

The few survivors became scattered among other southeastern tribes and were looked upon as wise and gifted with mystic power. As did the ancient sages of the other tribes, the Natchez had legendary tales of invaders from a region on the other side of the world. The Natchez described the mounds as the work of earlier people.

As the early exploration of America continued, there seemed to emerge mounting evidence of a civilization in the Americas that preceded the natives encountered by early explorers. The explanation for oddities such as a race of giants would require a reversal of a long-established intellectual and religious dogma. It seemed less of a task to continue to accept the belief that the Native Americans discovered by Christopher Columbus were the original mound builders. In 1881 the Smithsonian began to actively promote this idea, which today has found its way into the federal government's Department of Education as part of the elementary school curriculum. As a result the Smithsonian has been charged with effectively withholding information that supports the theoretical framework known as cultural diffusionism, which, as we have seen in chapter 1, is the simple and logical belief that throughout history people interacted via worldwide travels and trade.

While the Smithsonian may have spent the better part of a century manipulating research and selectively sequestering native artifacts to support the theory that the Mississippi Mound Builders were an otherwise unremarkable tribe, growing evidence points to the contrary.

During the 1800s the contents of many mounds were revealed to include the remains of huge men with estimated heights of seven or eight feet, buried in full copper armor with swords and axes. As settlers moved west, they came across and reported countless mounds. At the time it was not unusual to find stories or articles in local newspapers about discoveries of the remains of perfectly proportioned giants. As land was cleared for settlement and agriculture, some suggested that these mounds and their amazing contents were the products of ancient cultures that predated known native tribes. Tribes that greeted early pioneers told of a long-extinct race of giants.

Ohio historian Ross Hamilton explains:

The first hint we had about the possible existence of an actual race of tall, strong, and intellectually sophisticated people, was in researching Old Township and county records. Many of these were quoting from old diaries and letters that were combined, for posterity, in the 1800s from diaries going back to the 1700s. Some of these old county and regional history books contain real gems, because the people were not subjected to a rigid indoctrination about evolution and were astonished about what they found and honestly reported it.[3]

How did these bits of knowledge alluding to the existence of prehistoric races in the Americas get excluded from public education? Consider that prior to the establishment of the federal Department of Education, the Smithsonian Institution was looked upon as the guardian of the physical facts that have shaped our culture—the culture of a New World. At the time, the Smithsonian and its political and scientific endeavors were an outgrowth of the federal politics of the early 1800s, most notably struggles to deal with the so-called Indian problem, and struggles to justify the social costs of westward expansion. (The politics of the early 1800s, and the deadly consequences for Meriwether Lewis, are explained more fully in chapters 9 and 10.)

Government officials at the time of the Lewis and Clark expedition in 1804 considered the native occupation of the American continent to be the chief impediment to the creation of the New World. And while Thomas Jefferson is well known for being fascinated by and supportive of the so-called Indians, he also recognized that they represented a threat to westward expansion.

While Lewis and Clark were gathering information about native peoples and exploring potential trade routes west, Jefferson was developing a plan to get the natives out of the way—in what would later become a government policy known as Indian Removal.

The first component of his plan involved encouraging natives to adopt agricultural practices, which would reduce their territorial hunting areas. He hoped then that government agents would be able to convince natives to sell their surplus land.

The second component was an amplification of the first and involved encouraging natives to adopt a European-style agricultural economy in hopes that they would become dependent on trade with European settlers. That dependence, in turn, could be used as leverage against natives who resisted selling their land.

The third component of his plan involved establishing government trading posts near native settlements. His hope, in this case, was that natives could be fooled into spending themselves into debt. That debt, in turn, would be forgiven in exchange for tribal lands, which would be appropriated by the federal government.

Many tribes, including members of the Choctaw, Creek, and Cherokee tribes, willfully adopted European culture. They assimilated thoroughly, building schools and churches and creating government structures that resembled those of the United States of America. But Jefferson and agents of the American government met with increasing resistance from other tribes.

In 1803—the same year that the Louisiana Purchase was announced, and the same year that Lewis was chosen as the leader of the westward expedition—Jefferson sent a letter to the then governor of the Indiana Territory, William Henry Harrison, outlining his plan for removing the remaining resistant natives.

To promote this disposition to exchange lands, which they have to spare and we want, for necessaries, which we have to spare and they want, we shall push our trading uses, and be glad to see the good and influential individuals among them run in debt, because we observe that when these debts get beyond what the individuals can pay, they become willing to lop them off by a cession of lands. . . . In this way our settlements will gradually circumscribe and approach

Thomas Jefferson envisioned Louisiana Territory as a core component of his plans to remove natives from their lands.

the Indians, and they will in time either incorporate with us as citizens of the United States, or remove beyond the Mississippi. The former is certainly the termination of their history most happy for themselves; but, in the whole course of this, it is essential to cultivate their love. As to their fear, we presume that our strength and their weakness is now so visible that they must see we have only to shut our hand to crush them, and that all our liberalities to them proceed from motives of pure humanity only. Should any tribe be foolhardy enough to take up the hatchet at any time, the seizing the whole country of that tribe, and driving them across the Mississippi, as the only condition of peace, would be an example to others, and a furtherance of our final consolidation.[4]

This letter outlines that last part of Jefferson's grand design, which included a notion that would become known as land exchange; this involved trading tribal land in the eastern portion of the continent for land west of the Mississippi—what was then known as the Louisiana Territory (soon to become the Louisiana Purchase). Later, this practice would become the conceptual foundation for the Indian Removal Act of 1830.

Jefferson declared his intentions to use the Louisiana Territory as a dumping ground for displaced natives clearly in a letter to John C. Breckinridge during the summer of 1803.

The best use we can make of the country for some time, will be to give establishments in it to the Indians on the East side of the Missipi, in exchange for their present country, and open land offices in the last, & thus make this acquisition the means of filling up the Eastern side, instead of drawing off its population.[5]

Although Jefferson also had been a vocal proponent of natives' nobility, intelligence, and equality for decades, his philosophical perspectives were seemingly trumped by his political ambitions and pervasive

Eurocentric myopia. It was those same political ambitions that encouraged Jefferson to send Lewis west, both as an emissary and as a scout. It also follows that Lewis's appointment as governor of the Louisiana Territory was, at least in part, granted because Lewis had spent years studying and negotiating with native tribes. He was well suited for overseeing the task of relocating tribes to their new "homes" in Louisiana. As a seasoned naturalist, he also was well suited for overseeing the various tribes' training in European-style agricultural practices.

Jefferson's move to "civilize" the natives out of their land, and some of the scientific theories that he ascribed to, would later evolve into a doctrine known as Progressive Social Evolutionary Theory, taken up by one John Wesley Powell, who would come to exert great influence over United States public policy as head of several government agencies.

Powell began to exert real influence beginning in 1879, when he was named director of the Smithsonian Institution's Bureau of American Ethnology, which he helped create.

Like Jefferson and other "enlightened" predecessors, Powell held seemingly contradictory beliefs about the native peoples of America. Powell had been an ardent defender of native peoples, lived and worked among them, and worked tirelessly to preserve their culture and lands. It was this pursuit that led Powell to lobby Congress to change the way federal agencies dealt with land acquisition. In the process, he laid the groundwork for the creation of the United States Geological Survey and the Smithsonian Institution's Bureau of American Ethnology. This monumental task consolidated a number of government agencies that were previously under control of the United States Department of the Interior. It also created a phenomenal political power base for Powell and his associates in the scientific community.

By 1879 work begun by Jefferson and Lewis, including the study of native cultures and efforts to assimilate seemingly beloved natives into Euro-American culture, had become an official government mandate. Powell was now at the helm of the Bureau of American Ethnology, a member of the House Appropriations Committee, and also strongly allied with the National Academy of Sciences. He had grown from being a man in the field to being a member of the establishment, and given his new status, he went along with the mandate.

Like Jefferson, Powell made countless moral concessions in order to be able to continue his work. Those concessions included modifying, or perhaps ultimately coming clean about, his philosophical and scientific prejudices. Put simply, Powell was, at heart, and at the end of the day, a racist; he believed that natives, while fascinating in their own right, were inherently inferior to Europeans. This belief, championed by the emerging science dubbed ethnology, and later anthropology, became a pseudoscientific and philosophical justification for the decimation of native tribes, the plundering of natural resources, and the ever-growing list of horrific consequences of westward expansion begun by Jefferson and Lewis.

Lee Baker, professor of cultural anthropology and African American studies at Duke University, summarizes:

> Industrializing America . . . needed to explain the calamities created by unbridled westward, overseas, and industrial expansion. Although expansion created wealth and prosperity for some, it contributed to conditions that fostered rampant child labor, infectious disease, and desperate poverty. As well, this period saw a sharp increase in lynchings and the decimation of Native American lives and land. The daily experience of squalid conditions and sheer terror made many Americans realize the contradictions between industrial capitalism and the democratic ideals of equality, freedom, and justice for all. Legislators, university boards, and magazine moguls found it useful to explain this ideological crisis in terms of a natural hierarchy of class and race caused by a struggle for existence wherein the fittest individuals or races advanced while the inferior became eclipsed.
>
> Professional anthropology emerged in the midst of this crisis, and the people who used anthropology to justify racism, in turn, provided the institutional foundations for the field. By the last

decade of the nineteenth century, college departments, professional organizations, and specialized journals were established for anthropology. The study of "primitive races of mankind" became comparable to geology and physics. These institutional apparatuses, along with powerful representatives in the American Association for the Advancement of Science (AAAS), prestigious universities, and the Smithsonian Institution, gave anthropology its academic credentials as a discipline in the United States. The budding discipline gained power and prestige because ethnologists articulated theory and research that resonated with the dominant discourse on race.[6]

In an article written for *American Anthropologist* in 1888, titled "From Barbarism to Civilization," Powell made his views about natives and the so-called Indian Problem very clear: "In setting forth the evolution of barbarism to civilization, it becomes necessary to confine the exposition . . . to one great stock of people—the Aryan Race."[7]

This view—that native and African American races were inherently inferior to Europeans—became institutionalized thanks to Powell and powerful allies of his, including Powell's mentor, ethnologist, lawyer, senator, and railroad baron Lewis Henry Morgan; finance lord and museum magnate George Foster Peabody; publisher, AAAS president, and key developer of the Department of Anthropology at the American Museum of Natural History Frederic Ward Putnam; and influential educator Nathaniel Shaler, who worked tirelessly to produce scientific rationale for segregation and mistreatment of African Americans.

The views created by these so-called vanguards of cultural study persist, and only now have begun to unravel in the face of modern inquiry. In fact, during the past several decades, archaeological and ethnic studies have eroded, and in some cases obliterated, the notion that natives of the American continents were simple folk who lived in perfect harmony with the land around them. Authors such as Jared Diamond and Charles Mann, for example, have collected and presented evidence that natives molded and shaped the land, created technologies and systems of government, institutions, advanced agricultural practices, public sanitation, plumbing and other artifacts previously believed to be the sole province of non-natives.

In his book *1491: New Revelations of the Americas Before Columbus,* Mann notes that there is a

cohort of scholars that in recent years has radically challenged conventional notions of what the Western Hemisphere was like before Columbus. When I went to high school, in the 1970s, I was taught that Indians came to the Americas across the Bering Strait about thirteen thousand years ago, that they lived for the most part in small, isolated groups, and that they had so little impact on their environment that even after millennia of habitation that continents remained mostly wilderness. Schools still impart the same ideas today. One way to summarize the views . . . would be to say that . . . this picture of Indian life is wrong in almost every aspect. Indians were here far longer than previously thought, these researchers believe, and in much greater numbers. And they were so successful at imposing their will on the landscape that in 1492 Columbus set foot in a hemisphere thoroughly marked by humankind . . . some researchers—many but not all from an older generation—deride the new theories as fantasies arising from an almost willful misinterpretation of data and a perverse kind of political correctness.[8]

Mann quotes the Smithsonian Institution's Betty J. Meggers in relating a conversation about the Beni, a remote province in Bolivia that is host to a unique matrix of forest islands and mounds linked by causeways built by what many scholars believe to have been a vast, technologically advanced culture that inhabited the region.

"I have seen no evidence that large numbers of people ever lived in Beni," Meggers once told Mann. "Claiming otherwise is just wishful thinking."[9]

From this reasoning stems a view that Mann dubs "Holmberg's

Mistake," after Allan R. Holmberg, a young doctoral student who studied the best-known of the Beni-region natives, the Siriono, during the early 1940s.

The Siriono, Holmberg wrote in an account of his studies titled *Nomads of the Longbow*, were "among the most culturally backward peoples of the world." They were poor and impoverished, lived without clothes, had no domestic animals, no musical instruments, no art or design, and no discernable religion. They were, from Holmberg's perspective, living evidence of the failure of aboriginal culture to thrive and a justification of so-called civilized European influence. They were, he wrote, the "quintessence" of "man in the raw state of nature."[10] Holmberg also believed that this was the state the Siriono lived in for thousands of years. That is, until they encountered Spanish explorers and stepped into the river of modern history.

"Holmberg was a careful and compassionate researcher whose detailed observations of Siriono life remain valuable today," writes Mann. ". . . Nonetheless, he was wrong about the Siriono. And he was wrong about the Beni, the place they inhabited—wrong in a way that is instructive, even exemplary."[11]

Like Powell and other misguided founders of modern archaeology and anthropology, Holmberg neglected to consider more recent influences on the character and state of native culture. The Siriono, it was later surmised, were not a dead culture left over from antiquity but the remnants of an amazingly sophisticated culture that had been wiped out by smallpox and influenza in the 1920s. Some 95 percent of the Siriono, he neglected to consider, had been killed by disease or thrown into prison camps by the Bolivian government at the behest of white cattle ranchers who were taking over the Beni.

The Beni was no anomaly. For almost five centuries, Holmberg's take—the supposition that Native Americans lived in an eternal, unhistoried state—held sway in scholarly work, and from there fanned out to high school text books, Hollywood movies, newspaper articles, environmental campaigns, romantic adventure books, and silk-screened T-shirts. It existed in many forms and was embraced by those who hated Indians and those who admired them. Holmberg's Mistake explained the colonists' view of most Indians as incurably vicious barbarians; its mirror image was the dreamy stereotype of the Indian as Noble Savage.[12]

It is here—in the myth of the Noble Savage—that we encounter the dark side of cultural diffusionism. It is important to note that while new evidence pointing to pre-Columbian contact in the Americas is fascinating, much of the discussion of pre-Columbian contact with various Anglo-Saxon, African, and Asian peoples has been used to denigrate natives as well.

Some scholars contend, for example, that modern diffusionist researchers have simply circled back around to an old view—that native people weren't able to develop their own, advanced technologies and systems and that discoveries of advanced civilization on the American continent must have emerged thanks to contact with more advanced outsiders at some point in antiquity. Like early American settlers, many diffusionist theorists have trouble accepting the notion that native peoples were able to create their own advanced infrastructure, technology, sciences, and systems. In the case of the diffusionist viewpoint, natives were simply innocent and pure, living in an idyllic, though mildly contemptible, peace with nature. Any advancement, technological or otherwise, must have been borrowed or stolen from more advanced, seafaring cultures such as the Phoenicians or the Welsh.

"Positive or negative," writes Mann, "in both images Indians lacked what social scientists call agency—they were not actors in their own right, but passive recipients of whatever windfalls or disasters happenstance put in their way."[13]

John Wesley Powell, it seems, fell victim to both perspectives during his career. Like Holmberg, long before he was a political powerhouse and champion of justifying America's genocidal westward expansion, Powell was a well-intentioned researcher and a friend of the native people. It was in this role that Powell, paradoxically enough, shunted exploration of the Mississippi Mounds into the narrow confines of independent inventionist theory, the antithesis of the diffusionist view.

Once appointed to lead the Smithsonian's Bureau of American Ethnology (BEA) in 1879, Powell began building his academic empire. Three years after his appointment as leader of the bureau, Powell hired Cyrus Thomas to carry out fieldwork and explorations of the Mississippi Mounds as head of the BEA's Eastern Mounds Division. Thomas, a minister and entomologist, was said to have believed that an ancient race was involved in building the mounds. But Powell, who had once explored the mounds, believed strongly that close ancestors of the region's native tribes had built them.

Powell may have initially been motivated by his sympathies for natives and railed against notions that an ancient race of Anglo-Saxon origin or some other nonnative race had built the mounds. Early settlers in the region had surmised that an ancient, "superior" race had built the mounds, presumably driven by the notion that so-called savage native tribes couldn't possibly have created the amazing structures, or the artifacts they found in them. This superior race was alternatively believed to be of Egyptian, Norwegian, Saxon, Indian, Greek, Israeli, Belgian, African, and Welsh origin, depending on who was asked. Many scholars and early settlers characterized Native Americans as late arrivals who had savagely wiped out the complex, ancient civilizations that had built the mounds. From this, early settlers decided they were justified in desecrating the mounds and building farms and homesteads on mound sites. They were, it was reasoned, simply taking back the land on behalf of more civilized nations that had once been wiped out by ancestors of the native tribes.

Like Jefferson, Lewis, and others, settlers in the region had used selective interpretation of scientific data to justify their political exploits. And like the amazing waterways overlooked by Holmberg, the Cahokia mounds were fascinating, but not fascinating enough to warrant reconsidering whether to exploit the land and people that created them.

The mounds generated so much public interest that the Bureau of American Ethnology dedicated a quarter of its budget to their exploration. That work, overseen by Thomas, spanned twelve years and produced massive amounts of data from work at more than two thousand sites. In 1894 Thomas produced a 700-page "Report on the Mound Explorations of the Bureau of Ethnology" as part of the *Twelfth Annual Report of the Bureau of American Ethnology to the Secretary of the Smithsonian Institution*. It began with the question on many people's minds: "Were the mounds built by the Indians?" Thomas concluded, in keeping with his superiors' wishes, that natives had indeed built the mounds.

We may never know the true answer to the question, thanks to Powell's seemingly benevolent, and later ironic, decision to reject all evidence that might contradict his assertion that early America had not been visited by any European, African, Middle Eastern, or any other non-Asiatic, nonnative peoples. Voluminous amounts of irreplaceable historical data were lost, destroyed, or misplaced as a result of this decision.

As author Ross Hamilton explains:

Armed with a self-created doctrine powered by ample funding, and with a little help later from the one-way door to the Smithsonian's inaccessible catacombs, the years that followed saw Powell and his underlings nearly succeed in the obliteration of the last notions of the legendary, mysterious, and antique class of mound building people, and for that matter, any people that didn't fit into the mold of his theory. This decision led to a wholesale plunder of mounds and caves. In the process, anything that fit into Powell's narrow paradigm of American history was kept, while everything that did not, met an inglorious end. Ancient civilizations built mounds from the Great Lakes to the Gulf of Mexico and from the Mississippi River to the Appalachian Mountains, but the greatest concentrations of mounds are found in the Mississippi and Ohio River Valleys.[14]

Long before Powell arrived, the Corps of Discovery spent the winter of 1803–04 at a camp near the Cahokia Mounds, and both Lewis and Clark spent time exploring several of the more than 200 mounds that existed near their camp.

On September 10, 1803, Lewis visited the massive Grave Creek Mound, which is the largest mound of its kind, built from more than 60,000 tons of dirt. Construction of the mound took nearly a century, and resulted in a massive structure measuring 62 feet high and 240 feet in diameter.

The rain ceased about day, the clouds had not dispersed, and looked very much like giving us a repetition of the last evening's frollic, there was but little fogg and I should have been able to have set out at sunrise, but the Corporal had not yet returned with the bread—I began to fear that he was piqued with the sharp reprimand I gave him the evening before for his negligence and inattention with respect to the bread and had deserted; in this however I was agreably disappointed, about 8 in the morning he came up bring[ing] with him the two men and the bread, they instantly embarked and we set out we passed several very bad riffles this morning and at 11 Oclock six miles below our encampment of last evening I landed on the east side of the [river] and went on shore to view a remarkable artificial mound of earth called by the people in the neighbourhood the Indian grave. This remarkable artificial mound of earth stands on the east bank of the Ohio 12 Miles below Wheeling and about 700 paces from the river, as the land is not cleard the mound is not visible from the river—this mound gives name to two small creek called little and big grave creek which passing about a half a mile on each side of it and fall into ohio about a mile distant from each other the small creek is above, the mound stands on the most elivated ground of a large bottom containing about 4000 acres of land the bottom is bounded from N. E. to S. W. by a high range of hills which seem to discribe a simecircle around it of which the river is the dimater, the hills being more distant from the mound than the river, near the mound to the N. stands a small town lately laid out called Elizabethtown there are but six or seven dwelling houses in it as yet, in this town there are several mounds of the same kind of the large one but not near as large, in various parts of this bottom the traces of old intrenchments are to seen tho' they are so imperfect that they cannot be traced in such manner as to make any complete figure; for this enquire I had not leasure I shall therefore content myself by giving a discription of the large mound and offering some conjectures with regard to the probable purposes for which they were intended by their founders; who ever they may have been. the mound is nearly a regular cone 310 yards in circumpherence at its base and 65 feet high terminating in a blont point whose diameter is 30 feet, this point is concave being depresed about five feet in the center, arround the base runs a ditch 60 feet in width which is bro-ken or inte[r]sected by a ledge of earth raised as high as the outer bank of the ditch on the N. W. side, this bank is about 30 feet wide and appers to have formed the enterence to fortifyed mound—near the summit of this mound grows a white oak tree whose girth is 13½ feet, from the aged appeance of this tree I think it's age might resonably [be] calculated at 300 years, the whole mound is covered with large timber, sugar tree, hickery, poplar, red and white oak and c—I was informed that in removing the earth of a part of one of these lesser mounds that stands in the town the skeletons of two men were found and some brass beads were found among the earth near these bones, my informant told me the beads were sent to Mr Peals museum in Philadelphia where he believed they now were. . . .[15]

Strangely, the remaining half page and five following pages of Lewis's description of the mound were left blank for reasons that remain unexplained.

Spirit Mound inspired Lewis and Clark to take an eleven-man team to explore the solitary, strange-looking hill that was said at the time to be inhabited by armed, strange, eighteen-inch-tall "little devils" with large heads. The hill, dubbed Paha Wakan by the Sioux, was a source of awe to the Omaha, Sioux, and Otoes tribes, which believed that the mound was occupied by spirits that would kill any human that approached it. *The Journals of Lewis and Clark* contain the first written records of Spirit Mound, which the Corps of Discovery explored on August 24, 1804. Clark writes,

> Capt Lewis and my Self Concluded to visit a High Hill Situated in an emence Plain three Leagues N. 20° W. from the mouth of White Stone river, this hill appear to be of a Conic form and by all the different Nations in this quater is Supposed to be a place of Deavels or that they are in human form with remarkable large heads and about 18 inches high; that they are very watchfull and ar armed with Sharp arrows with which they can kill at a great distance; they are said to kill all persons who are so hardy as to attemp to approach the hill; they state that tradition informs them than many indians have suffered by these little people and among others that three Maha men fell a sacrefice to their murcyless fury not meany years since so much do the Mahas Souix Ottoes and other neibhbouring nations believe this fable that no consideration is sufficient to induce them to approach this hill.[16]

Many scholars dismiss Clark's stories of these "little demons" as tales of a failed attempt to prove a primitive legend. But some, such as Dr. Robert Saindon, suggest that Lewis and Clark may have ventured into a realm that was once inhabited by honest-to-god mystical dwarves. As late as 1977 newspaper articles in the *Billings Gazette* mention discoveries of curious, diminutive, mummified remains discovered by locals. One mummy, discovered by gold prospectors in the Pedro Mountains, displayed bronze skin, a low forehead, a flat nose, a full set of teeth, and eerie eyes. X-rays of the tiny mummy revealed human vertebrae and a typical, though smaller, adult human skeletal structure.

One article cited by Saindon suggests that native legends of the little people indicate the mummified remains may have been nearly 10,000 years old and that similar skeletons and mummies have been found as far north as Yellowstone and in caves near the Colorado border.[17]

Also steeped in mystery and legend, Ohio's Great Serpent Mound is by far the largest and most interesting serpentine effigy mound in the world. Ohio archaeologist Dr. William F. Romain, who studied the mound for decades, writes:

> The Serpent Mound acropolis is located in a 7–8 mile wide peninsula of unglaciated Lexington Plain, also known as Ohio Bluegrass, that intrudes between unglaciated Appalachian plateau on the east, and glaciated Till Plain on the west. In layman's terms, Serpent Mound was strategically placed to command a view of the foothills of the Appalachian Mountains to the east, and the open, fertile plains in the west. The Serpent Mound acropolis also sits in a narrow region of Mixed Mesophytic forest, bordered by Oak, Sugar Maple and Beech forests. Mixed Mesophytic forests are a remnant of the type of forest that once covered North America in ancient times. They are made up of a wide variety of trees and plant life including primarily Sugar Maple, Buckeye, Basswood and Red Oak, as well as Big-Leaf Magnolia, American Beech, and Euonymus. The soil is rich and undisturbed, not too dry and not too moist, and tends to be more acidic. This type of forest is fast disappearing, now remaining only in the eastern United States and in eastern and central China.
>
> The Serpent Mound also lies near the intersection of several fault lines, and in an area of unusual magnetic activity, combined with an area of unusually intense gravity anomalies. In all the areas where the mounds are located are a collection of natural and artificial lakes. On the shores of these lakes the natives built vast cities. The cities were circular in shape and surrounded by walls. Behind the

walls, inhabitants carved out large canals to enable the waters of the lake or river to enter.[18]

These canals provided them with an inexhaustible supply of fresh water and made it possible for them to maintain a year-round supply of live fish. The canals also provided transportation.

With amazing skill, the engineers developed an internal system of navigation, linking the lakes and rivers with the various metropolitan centers of the region. It also was via these interconnecting waterways that the cities received needed produce. The Mississippi River served as the principal transportation artery. Many archaeologists and investigators agree that the artificial rivers in the southern part of the United States are a gift handed down by the pre-Columbian ancestors of the region.

Old public county documents of the diaries and letters of early settlers mention the unearthing of giant bones in land being developed.

Today we may not know who the Mound Builders were, but the answer may have been known two hundred years ago. As previously described, as time went on, stories like these were actively suppressed by ruling factions of the government who were interested in presenting a different view of the history of America. What would Meriwether Lewis's ongoing role in all of this be?

Four

Lewis and Clark and the Journey West

Thomas Jefferson was known to have in his own personal library the most accurate and complete collection of books and maps cataloging the West. His father, Peter Jefferson, was a skilled cartographer and surveyor. In Virginia surveyors enjoyed prominent status and had plenty of opportunity to become landowners as well. Anyone who wanted to obtain title to an area of land had to deal with a surveyor. In many cases, a surveyor's knowledge of the land would garner him employment representing large land companies. Surveyors were also among the best-educated Virginians, and it was not unusual for them to acquire large estates from the opportunities afforded by their profession.

Before 1755 the lands west along the Allegheny Mountains had not been settled. Land ownership in Virginia was necessary for the settlement of the area and for the growing prosperity of the colonial planter. The colonies were thriving, and the assurance of westward expansion depended largely on the incentive of land ownership. The expansion west was not just expected. It was being carefully laid out.

People settling in what was known then as the Northern Neck were required to obtain a survey warrant from the Northern Neck Proprietary Office for a set amount of acreage in a specific location.

The survey warrant, issued directly from the office to the county sur-veyor, instructed the surveyor to make a "just and true" survey of the land, officially determining and limiting its boundaries.

In 1749 Peter Jefferson founded the Loyal Land Company of Virginia along with another fellow Virginian and close neighbor, Thomas Meriwether, Lewis's grandfather. The Loyal Land Company was formed to petition for grants of land west of the Allegheny Mountains. In addition to Peter Jefferson and Thomas Meriwether, the Loyal Land Company included other members and families of high influence, magnates, and large landowners.

The Loyal Land Company of Virginia received 800,000 acres in 1749. They had plans to fund expeditions west in 1753, just four years after forming the company. The quest unfortunately had to be abandoned indefinitely when the French and Indian War broke out. Peter Jefferson never realized his dream of exploring the West. He died on the family ranch and left his large estate to his fourteen-year-old son Thomas.

Immediately after his father's death, Jefferson began attending what was considered the finest school in Albemarle County, Virginia, under the tutelage of Rev. James Maury. Maury was known in the area as a great teacher of classic education, such as morals and manners, history, literature, mathematics, and geography, which he considered essential in the education of a "well rounded" young man. The clergyman also pro-moted settling the West. Most of the boys attending the school boarded there because it was too far to come and go each day from home.

Consequently, strong friendships were formed. Many of the young men educated by Reverend Maury would go on to become great person-ages in the molding of the new country. Thomas Jefferson lived with the minister and his family for two years, and the influence Maury had on the young Jefferson is evident in the latter's passion for geogra-phy and the exploration of the West. It was a passion Jefferson main-tained even as his political career evolved steadily from governor, vice president, to president. It is worth noting that another future president, James Madison, had been a pupil of Reverend Maury.

In 1784 Jefferson introduced to Congress an ordinance that allowed new states to be formed from western territories. Much of Jefferson's excitement about possible trade routes and passages west rested on maps of the American continent produced by early French explorers. It is important to note that maps of America were based almost entirely on conjecture and stemmed from pseudoscientific theories that were equal parts analysis and wishful thinking. Jefferson subscribed to one of these theories, known as Symmetrical Geography, which suggested that the topography of the western American continent mirrored the eastern half—literally that mountains, rivers, and waterways of the eastern and western portions of America were identical, or at least remarkably similar. This theory included a belief in the so-called Long River, which was thought to comprise a series of interlocking lakes and rivers that would provide a water route west. The Long River legend was later replaced by a belief in two rivers running east and west that converged to create a waterway that would be able to carry explorers to the Pacific Ocean.

In a time when most of the population lived within forty miles of the Atlantic Ocean, Congress disapproved of allowing newly discovered lands to be given status equal to that of the original states. Undeterred, Jefferson helped sponsor the French botanist André Michaux in hopes of finding the quickest route to the Pacific Ocean. This expedition collapsed near the Mississippi, suffering from political conspiracies and paranoia.

The French, Spanish, and Native Americans were fighting westward expansion, but Jefferson pressed on with a steady resolve. He had a number of interests and was endlessly studying, never resting, knowing that Great Britain or any other nation could claim land on the soil he and his Revolutionary War brethren fought to protect.

In the beginning of 1801, with the help of the American Philosophical Society, an institution for knowledge created by Benjamin Franklin, Jefferson finally took the first real steps westward.

He chose his private secretary and personal protégé, Meriwether Lewis, to lead the expedition.

Lewis was sent to Philadelphia, where he personally studied under some of the sharpest minds of his time. The preparation called for an intensive review of botany, mathematics, chemistry, anatomy, and medicine. It is not difficult to imagine Lewis readying himself for this important mission, comparing himself with the Spanish conquistadores, stockpiling rifles and ammunition, and securing the proper instruments and equipment.

The taking and collection of notes on newly discovered plants, animals, and minerals was of great importance, as was disciplined documentation of all discoveries in journals. Lewis was well prepared for the task and had a strong personal bond to Jefferson. Both came from the same neighborhood in Virginia and were pioneering sons of distinguished families. Jefferson practically watched Lewis grow up.

Born on the family farm August 18, 1774, Meriwether Lewis had lived just miles from Jefferson's Monticello. Lewis was born to parents of high prominence in central Virginia. Thomas Jefferson had two siblings that married into the Lewis family, and Meriwether's uncle had handled Jefferson's relations during his years of diplomatic service in Paris. When Meriwether was five, his father died of pneumonia. His mother remarried, moving the entire family south to Georgia. It was during that time Lewis developed his skills as a tracker, herb gatherer, and outdoorsman. Hunting at night alone with his dogs, the ten-year-old Lewis developed a lifelong passion for the earth's natural wonders. It was in Georgia that Lewis had his first encounter with the Cherokees. Even as a curious young boy, Lewis was sensitive to the plight of the natives.

Meriwether returned to Virginia in his early teens to be educated. But when he finished his formal schooling, he opted to return to the family farm rather than continue on to college. His scheme to spend time expanding his land and growing his own flora and herbs was short-lived. Trouble brewed as new taxes on whiskey caused farmers to rebel. Riots spread in the colonies. During August 1794, President Washington mobilized thirteen thousand militiamen from Virginia, New Jersey, Pennsylvania, and Maryland. Lewis, who was worried about the safety of his land, quickly enlisted. The revolt was uneventful and quickly suppressed. Lewis, however, had found some excitement in the promise of travel and decided to remain with the army. Serving under General Wayne during the Battle of Fallen Timbers, Lewis arrived after the slaughter just in time for the signing of the Treaty of Greenville. The landmark treaty was a success for the western confederacy but a sad loss for the Native Americans who turned over Ohio, the future site of downtown Chicago, and Fort Detroit. It was during this military campaign that Lewis met William Clark for the first time. The two instantly forged a deep bond.

Lewis was the consummate adventurer—curious, strong, smart, artistically inclined, and fearless. He was as comfortable in battle as he was in the laboratory, in the library, or in the field. At heart he was a soldier and an adventurer, but he had spent so much time in the company of learned men like Jefferson that his rough edges had been refined. Lewis also was known for mood swings and occasional fits of melancholy. He is alternatively described by various biographers as sensitive, brash, self-aware, poetic, driven, depressed, fearless, and easily angered. He was also characterized as hard to get along with and seems to have held many of the racist tendencies that characterized men of his day. His treatment of Sacagawea, for example, was often described as condescending and dismissive.

Clark was also born in Virginia, the ninth of ten children from English and Scottish ancestry. Unlike the Lewis family, the Clarks did not have a drop of aristocratic blood. As with most children of his era, Clark was home-schooled. Shy, awkward, and self-conscious, he preferred reading books to socializing. At fifteen, his family moved to Kentucky, where Clark ultimately would break out of his shell. Learning wilderness survival tactics, he began to prepare for his inevitable calling. Clark had five older brothers, all with hardened military experience. He understood he would have to follow in his brothers' footsteps to gain respect. That was no easy task, considering that one of his brothers was a general during the American Revolutionary War.

Clark's childhood home was a battlefield, under constant raids by the Wea natives. At nineteen years old William Clark began his military career by volunteering to help push tribes out of Kentucky in order to secure the Ohio River. Kentucky militia made no effort to distinguish between warring and peaceful tribes, a point made clear by the attack on the peaceful Shawnee. Appalled by the murder of women and children, Clark detailed these horrors in his journal. Rising up the ranks to lieutenant, he proved to be a good soldier, showing his unmatched expertise in mapping and tracking new lands while commanding troops and winning battles. He was praised for his leadership. But after seven years, the harshness of nonstop conflicts took their toll and Clark prematurely retired, claiming poor health.

As Clark's military career dipped, his friend Meriwether Lewis seemed to be rocketing straight to the top. After six years in military service Lewis was promoted to the rank of captain. A year later he was invited by Thomas Jefferson, the newly elected president, to be his private secretary. It was a role he happily accepted. After convincing Congress, Jefferson's plan for exploring the West was set in motion. Lewis, who had been preparing for this journey for what seemed his whole life, was now on the verge of final reckoning. He knew that such a dangerous expedition demanded the preparedness and skills of an equal.

Lewis sought his good friend William Clark, writing him a letter and promising Clark would be his co-captain. The letter enthusiastically detailed the importance of the expedition. An exciting adventure and a chance to be the first to see the Pacific Ocean from land was an offer too good to refuse. It appears, in Clark's case, that venturing into the unknown with one of his friends, and getting paid to do so, was the right remedy for a man who had abandoned military life. After weeks passed with no response, Lewis was ready to move on when he finally received news that Clark indeed would be joining the party. The newly created Corps of Discovery was setting off on a mission as important in its time as the moon launch was for us in ours.

Left Pittsburgh this day at 11 o'clock with a party of 11 hands 7 of which are soldiers, a pilot and three young men on trial they having proposed to go with me throughout the voyage.

—AUGUST 31, 1803[1]

So began the first journal entry as Lewis departed Elizabeth, Pennsylvania, on his magnificently crafted 55-foot-long keelboat. The boat was narrow and fast, designed to move people swiftly upriver. Almost immediately Lewis was confronted with scientific curiosities. At Big Bone Lick, Kentucky, Lewis helped assist Dr. William Goforth excavate fossil remains of a mastodon. After five days spent studying and cataloging this find, Lewis sent his first shipment of specimens back to President Jefferson. Jefferson was an avid mastodon-bone collector and believed they were not extinct. Lewis was told to keep an eye out for this elusive creature in the unexplored western territories. So impressed were the revolutionary forefathers they went as far as proclaiming the mighty mastodon as America's national symbol.

In December 1803, William Clark took the responsibility of training the men who had volunteered to go to the Pacific. In a camp set up near present-day Hartford, Illinois, he began the task of building a cooperative and trail-fit team. It was a challenge, considering most of the men had never met one another. Clark taught them to build forts out of logs, to march in formation, and to use their weapons effectively. The dangers they expected to face were numerous, and they prepared skillfully for every possible scenario.

In early 1804 Meriwether Lewis attended the ceremony in which the Upper Louisiana Territory was transferred to the United States. In the most awesome real estate deal in history, the United States took control of a vast territory covering 828,800 square miles encompassing present-day Arkansas, Missouri, Iowa, Oklahoma, Kansas, Nebraska, parts of Minnesota west of the Mississippi River, most of North Dakota, nearly all of South Dakota, northeastern New Mexico, portions of Montana, Wyoming, and Colorado east of the Continental Divide, and Louisiana west of the Mississippi River, including the city of New Orleans and parts of the Canadian provinces of Alberta and Saskatchewan.

In May of 1804 William Clark, the newly formed Corps of Discovery, and Meriwether Lewis met at St. Charles, Missouri. The assembled party of forty-five included twenty-seven unmarried soldiers, a French interpreter, Captain Lewis's beloved dog Seaman, and another group of soldiers who would accompany them to Mandan country during the first winter of the expedition. Even French boatmen were recruited to help manage the boats, which were laden with supplies.

The expedition's first few months were a rough trial. As the group traveled up the Missouri River, they were beset with injuries, bitten relentlessly by insects, and beaten down by persistent heat. In August 1804 the Corps of Discovery lost a man to appendicitis. Fortunately it would turn out to be the only casualty of the mission. Along their path they came across huge logs and trees that bore witness to the storms and strong currents of the area. This made parts of the journey difficult, as these floating obstacles could damage and sink the boats. During the worst of these stretches the only way to see the boats safely through was to have the men pull the boat upriver using the cordelling technique, which requires boats to be pulled with ropes by men walking the shoreline. Averaging no more than ten or fifteen miles a day, the slow process was an additional frustration.

The first meetings with Native American tribes went smoothly. These were peaceful tribes on the outskirts of the territories. In preparation for these encounters, Lewis developed an introductory ceremony or brief ritual, in which, dressed in full uniform, they would inform the tribe's chief that their land now belonged to the United States and that a man in the East—President Thomas Jefferson—was their new "great father." They would also present the chief with a peace medal showing Jefferson on one side and two hands clasping on the other, as well as some form of present. In addition the corps members would perform a kind of parade, or presentation of arms, during which they would march in uniform and shoot their guns.

Lewis had been warned of the Teton Sioux. Sioux tribal members were fiercely aggressive when it came to their territory. The Sioux slept in tepees and hunted buffalo. These small bands of South Dakota warriors were feared among the French and Canadian traders. Neighboring tribes were no match for the Sioux's aggressiveness and were often slaughtered if they interfered. The Sioux were the fierce and demanding gatekeepers of the Missouri River. Controlling the traffic of the river, they demanded large amounts of gifts from passing merchants.

When Lewis arrived, tensions were thick. The ceremonial display didn't impress the Sioux, who knew the Americans sought control of the river. The Sioux demanded one of the boats from Lewis and Clark, and when this was denied, the tribe held the expedition hostage for three drama-filled days. The Sioux put on a war ceremony for them, complete with freshly scalped heads from the neighboring Omaha. The psychological warfare was unbelievable. Nobody in the expedition knew how to speak the Sioux language. The situation was a powder keg waiting to explode. Then, on the fourth day, Chief Black Buffalo of the Sioux granted Lewis and Clark's expedition safe passage in exchange for extra tobacco. Relieved that they had survived their first unexpected obstacle intact, Lewis and Clark were eager finally to be looking for something that was actually on their agenda.

The Missouri and Mississippi Valley area was home to thousands of mounds in prehistory. These mounds were of great curiosity to antiquarian thinkers of colonial America. Because they were believed to be more than just Native American burials, a closer investigation of these mounds was of high importance.

With several men and Lewis's dog Seaman, they hiked the miles from where they set up camp on the river. The four-hour hike took its toll on the explorers; they were completely overpowered by the heat. The dog returned to the river, and the men collapsed at the base of the mound in dire thirst. After rehydrating, Lewis and Clark climbed 70 feet to the top of Spirit Mound. They looked down on the impressive view and, seeing the entire valley plain from above for the first time, witnessed the wild buffalo roaming undisturbed. The Spirit Mound is one of the few remaining sites left standing from the original Lewis and Clark expedition. Jaw slack in amazement, Lewis made the following entry dated August 25, 1804.

> From the top of this Mound we beheld a most butifull landscape; Numerous herds of buffalow were Seen feeding in various directions, the Plain to the N. W & N E extends without interuption as far as Can be Seen— . . . no woods except on the Missouri Points. . . . If all the timber which is on the Stone Creek (Vermillion River) was on 100 acres it would not be thickly timbered, the Soil of those Plains are delightfull. Here we got Great quantities of the best large-set grapes I ever tasted, some Blue currents stil on the bushes, and two kinds of plumbs, one the Common wild Plumb the other a large Yellow Plumb . . . about double the Size of the Common and Deliscously flavoured.[2]

After Lewis and company returned to camp, they briefly considered hiking the lands beyond Spirit Mound but decided the heat would make it dangerous. They continued upriver the next morning and never looked back. If they had ventured just a little farther, they would have crossed paths with America's biggest pre-Columbian mystery.

The Cahokia Mounds are a gigantic complex settlement of ancient mounds that includes Monks Mound. The name *Cahokia* is attributed to an unrelated clan of Illiniwek people living in the area when the first French explorers arrived in the 1600s, long after Cahokia was abandoned by its original inhabitants. The living descendants of the Cahokia people associated with the mound site are unknown. French explorers assigned the name Cahokia in the late seventeenth century. The name stuck even though the natives claimed the mounds were much older than they were.

Best known for large, manmade earthen structures, the city of Cahokia was inhabited from about 700 to 1400 CE. Built by ancient peoples known casually as the Mound Builders, Cahokia's original population was thought to have been approximately 1,000 until about the eleventh century, when it expanded to tens of thousands.

At its apex, estimated between 1,100 to 1,200 CE, the city covered nearly six square miles and hosted a population of as many as a hundred thousand people.

These ancient natives are said to have built more than 120 earthen mounds in the city, 109 of which have been recorded and 68 of which are preserved within the site. While some are no more than a gentle rise on the land, others reach 100 feet into the sky. Natives are said to have transported the earthen material used to build the mounds on their backs in baskets to the construction sites. More than fifty million cubic feet of earth was moved for the construction of the mounds.

A rapid decline in the Cahokian population is said to have begun sometime after 1200 CE.

By 1400 CE the site heralded as hosting the most magnificent pre-Columbian city north of Mexico was barren. Theories abound as to what led to the seemingly catastrophic decline of the civilization, including war, disease, drought, and sudden climate change. Archaeologists scratch their heads when considering the fact that there are no legends, records, or mention of the magnificent city in the annals of other local tribes, including the Osage, Omaha, Ponca, and Quapaw.

The largest earthwork at the historical site, called Monks Mound, is at the center. At least 100 feet tall, it is the largest manmade, prehistoric mound in North America. The mound is 1,000 feet long, 800 feet wide, and composed of four platform terraces. Archaeologists estimated that 22 million cubic feet of earth was used to build the mound between the years of 900 and 1,200 CE. Since then the mound has eroded or been damaged to the point that no one knows how large the mound really was.

Even more curious than the existence and seemingly sudden disappearance of a vast culture is the surprising discovery of what appears to be a massive stone structure lying hidden below the massive Monks Mound.

On January 24, 1998, while drilling to construct a water drainage system at Monks Mound, workers hit a 32-foot-long stone structure.

"This is astounding," said William I. Woods, professor of geography and courtesy professor of anthropology at Kansas University, who was at the time an archaeologist with Southern Illinois University at Edwardsville. Woods led the investigation of the mystery structure. "The stone is at least 32 feet (10 meters) long in one of its dimensions," he wrote. "It is buried about 40 feet below the surface of a terrace on the western side of Monk's Mound and well above the mound's bottom."[3]

Woods noted that even if the structure turned out to be just a large slab of stone, it would still be a dramatic find, because the nearest source of stone was more than ten miles from Cahokia, which lies approximately twenty miles southeast of St. Louis. In fact, no stones had ever been found at the site other than those used to craft primitive tools, weapons, and artifacts.[4]

Archaeologists Andy Martignoni Jr. and Steve Fulton were on duty at the site and discussed the situation, speculating it could be a drain or even a tomb. Comparing the "feel" of the drill with countless other operations, the drill operator told them the structure seemed to be made of large stones apparently placed together deliberately, deep into the western face. That gave the archaeologists more reason to think this might be something other than just a large rock. There is a large region of stone of undetermined shape located 40 feet below one of the terrace surfaces but still well above the base of the mound. Until then the prevailing dogma has long been that the Native Americans who built Cahokia worked only with earth, never with stone, which is not found anywhere near the region in question. The Monks Mound discovery directly challenged thinking at the time about the culture that built Cahokia and suggests that what is beneath the mounds themselves may be much, much older. Discovery of the massive, unidentified stone could push the dates of construction back much further, associating Cahokia with other similar structures that range from 3,000 to 3,500 years of age.

More recently the discovery made at Cahokia on February 17, 2010, of what appears to have been a Stone Age copper workshop has baffled explorers even further. About two hundred yards east of Monks Mound, an excavation revealed evidence of the only known copper workshop from the Mississippian era. The copper workshop is being studied in relation to a peculiarity on an engraved drinking cup made from a conch shell found at the top of the 10-foot-high mound. Some speculate that the shell came from the Gulf of Mexico. It contains a symbol of an arrowlike logo with a circle in the arrowhead. This symbol first turned up in rock shelters excavated in Wisconsin and east central Missouri and was dated from about 1000 CE, more than two hundred years before the peak of Cahokia-area civilization.

The symbols on the shelter walls are similar to the shell fragments found on the mound at Cahokia, and scholars now believe Cahokia may have been the center of the ancient Mississippian culture. Copper relics have been found throughout the Mississippi Mound network, but to claim that they all must be related somehow to the Cahokias is too hasty an assumption. Could these earth-covered mounds conceal the remains of much older and forgotten ruins? The truth will be revealed only when a full dig is conducted. As it is today, less than 1 percent of the Cahokia mounds have been excavated. What is ironic about the copper find is that this recent excavation did not take place at the site of the stone structure but rather somewhere else leading to an even more fascinating discovery.

And while Lewis didn't get to see all of Cahokia, he and the party did wander into the mounds at Grave Creek. After Lewis's vivid descriptions of these mounds in his journal and his documentation of finding brass beads in a burial site, the journal is abruptly cut off. It remains unexplained why everything in the journals of Lewis is detailed meticulously until the topic of mounds is mentioned. Then begins a series of strange omissions or missing pages. Gary Moulton elaborates.

More difficult to explain is Lewis's lack of journal-keeping once the expedition got underway. No Lewis journals are known to exist that cover the first phase of the expedition, from May 14, 1804, until the group left Fort Mandan on April 7, 1805. This is the longest hiatus in Lewis's writing and to historians it is the most curious gap.[5]

This gap, and others, are discussed further in chapter 9.

Above the surface, scholars teach that the mounds are the works of the Native Americans. But below the surface another tale is emerging as a growing number of scholars come forth with evidence that points to a prehistoric civilization that predates the Native American.

Five

Prince Madoc, Welsh Natives, and Legends of the Mandan

During their encounter with the Flathead (Salish) Indians on September 5, 1805, while in what is today western Montana, members of the Corps of Discovery noted that the natives spoke a strange tongue. Sergeant John Ordway observed, "these natives have the Stranges language of any we have ever seen. they appear to us as though they had an Impedement in their Speech or brogue on their tongue. we think perhaps that they are the welch Indians."[1] Clark noted in his journal that only the Flathead (Salish) tongue was "a gugling kind of language Spoken much through the Throught."[2]

Ordway was certain the Corps had discovered the legendary Welsh Indians descended from Welsh Prince Madoc, who had sailed to the American continent centuries before Columbus. As the story goes, in 1170 CE a Welsh prince named Madoc sailed west, far away from the disasters occurring in his homeland. Bards throughout the next four centuries did the same. The earliest printed report of Madoc's story is David Powel's *The History of Cambria,* published in 1584.

Madoc . . . left the land in contention betwixt his brethrens and pre-pared certain ships with men and munitions and sought adventures by seas, sailing west. . . He came to a land unknown where he saw many strange things. . . . Of the visage and returned of this Madoc there be many fables, as the common people do use in distance of place and length of time, rather to augment than diminish; but sure it is that there he was. . . . And after he had returned home, and declared the pleasant and fruitful countries that he had seen, he pre-pared a number of ships, and got with him such men and women as were desirous to live in quietness, and taking leave of his friends took his journey thitherward again. Madoc arriving in the country, into which he came in the year 1170, left most of his people there, and returning back for more of his own nation, acquaintance, and friends, to inhabit that fair and large country, went thither again.[3]

Gutyn Owen, the famous bard and historian of Basingwerk Abbey. is one of the most influential proprietors of the Madoc myth. His writings are cited as crucial sources by authors such as Richard Deacon, who wrote the influential *Madoc and the Discovery of America* in 1966. This rare book builds a solid case for Madoc's voyage of discovery, despite controversial claims that Madoc's story was invented after 1492, giving England claim to prior rights in the New World. Deacon's research indicates that in 1625 the archbishop of Canterbury wrote a world history that suggested a Welsh prince had discovered America. What if the young Prince Madoc lived on to build ancient settlements and interact with the Native Americans? The ocean current naturally would have carried Madoc and his fleet into the Gulf of Mexico. Once there he would have been attracted to the perfect harbor offered in Mobile Bay.

There's another traveler the ancient bards speak of who also sailed to American shores. An Irish monk named St. Brendan was said to have discovered sometime between 512 and 530 CE an island so big he failed to find the shore after forty days of walking in a forested land full of fresh fruits and divided by a river too wide to cross. His tales, first published in Latin, were fanciful bestsellers that read more like great entertainment than actual reality. St. Brendan's exploits were quickly synchronized with folklore, and he joined Madoc as another mythological hero. In 1977 historian, author, and ship captain Tim Severin proved a voyage from Ireland to the North American mainland was possible. Against all odds Severin and his robust crew built a leather boat exactly like those used in the days of St. Brendan and sailed across the dangerous Atlantic Ocean, safely landing in Newfoundland.

There have been ancient fortifications found along the Mississippi River, with architecture unlike any previously discovered in the region. In a 1781 letter, Governor John Seiver of Tennessee recounts a conversation he had with a ninety-year-old Cherokee chief. Seiver asked the chief about the people who had left the fortifications in his country. The chief told him white people who crossed the Great Water had built them. This letter can be found in the files of the Georgia Historical Commission.

There are three major forts that stand out against the typical native settlements found along the Mississippi. All three of these forts share striking similarities to ancient Welsh fortifications. The fort at Chatsworth, Georgia, is virtually identical in layout and method of construction to Dolwyddelan Castle in Wales, the supposed birthplace of Prince Madoc.

As forts were built and territory expanded upriver, a clash with hostile native tribes was inevitable. It's presumed this hostility forced them to build a defensive stronghold, complete with a massive wall 800 feet long. The wall, another anomaly of southeastern archaeology, long predates the Cherokees found living there in the 1700s. Cherokee legends called the wall builders "moon-eyed people," who were said to have fair skin, blond hair, and blue eyes. Throughout the centuries scholars and historians have argued for and against the Madoc story.

In November 1953 a memorial tablet was erected at Fort Morgan, Mobile Bay, Alabama, by the Virginia Cavalier Chapter of the Daughters of the American Revolution, which reads, "In memory of Prince Madoc, a Welsh explorer, who landed on the shores of Mobile Bay in 1170 and left behind, with the Indians, the Welsh language."

The memorial, subject to much controversy, was taken down after a hurricane in 1970. Despite resolutions being passed and the support of the governor to restore the plaque, this part of American history is mostly forgotten, covered up, or transparently ignored.

More than any other tribe, the Mandan of the northern plains showed signs of contact with Welsh explorers such as Madoc. They were a small, peaceful tribe that lived at the convergence of the Knife and Missouri Rivers near Bismarck, North Dakota. They were known for their friendliness, which was the outward expression of a deep-seated ethical philosophy. The Mandan shared the northern plains with tribes such as the Hidatsa, Arikara, Assiniboin, Dakota, and Chippewa. The lands they collectively inhabited were largely similar and had few natural barriers to prevent the mingling of people. Because of this the various tribes had many traits in common. They all depended on buffalo for food, clothing, and other necessities.

But of these, only the Mandan and Hidatsa lived in earth-lodge villages when they were first visited by white people in what is now North Dakota. The Mandan were further differentiated from their native counterparts in the way they set up their villages, their spiritual beliefs, and their physical appearance. These differences have led many scholars to suggest that the Mandan derived from different bloodlines than their northern plains counterparts. Despite a widespread absence of facts about the Mandan in history books, there is more than enough documentation elsewhere to suggest that the tribe originated in Europe.

The Mandan lived in earth-lodge homes rather than teepees, and unlike the settlements of other tribal nations, theirs were permanent. The women of the Mandan tribe tended their gardens, prepared food, and maintained the lodges while the men spent their time hunting or seeking spiritual knowledge. Their villages were strategically located on bluffs overlooking the river. This position provided maximum defense and limited any attacks to one land approach. These villages were the center of the social, spiritual, and economic lives of the Mandan.

The Mandan earth lodges were unlike those built by other tribes. These lodges were large rectangular and circular huts 15 feet high and 40 to 60 feet in diameter. Each hut had a vestibule entrance and a square hole on top that served as a smokestack. Each earth lodge housed ten to thirty people and their belongings. Villages contained fifty to one hundred earth lodges. The frame of an earth lodge was made from tree trunks, which were covered with crisscrossed willow branches. Over the branches they placed dirt and sod. This type of construction made the roofs strong enough to support people on nights of good weather. The floors of earth lodges were made of dirt, and the middle was dug out to make a bench around the outer edge of the lodge.

Surrounding the village were stockades of poles as tall as 6 feet high to prevent enemy attacks. In the middle of a Mandan village was a large, circular open space that was called the central plaza. In the middle of the plaza was a sacred cedar post that represented the "Ark of the First Man" or "Lone Man," a revered hero from their ancient legend. At the north end of the plaza was the medicine or ceremonial lodge. The arrangement of the lodges around the central plaza represented the social status of each family. The higher in status villagers were, the more duties were required of them, and therefore they were located closer to the ceremonial lodge. A strange feature of the Mandan villages that did not correspond with the behavior of other native tribes was that the Mandan homes were arranged resembling streets. The Hidatsas, another peaceful tribe, were the only other native people who built earthen huts, which practice they learned from the Mandan.

The rich flood-plain fields that surrounded the village made agriculture the basis of Mandan existence. The Mandan women were responsible for sustaining the gardens within the village. The agricultural year began in April when the women would clear the fields by burning the old stalks and weeds of the previous year's crops. Around May they planted rows of corn, beans, tobacco, pumpkin, sunflowers, and squash to maximize exposure to sunlight. To tend their gardens, women used tools such as digging sticks, rakes, and hoes made from wood or buffalo bones. To protect their gardens from natural predators like prairie dogs, birds, and rodents, the women constructed scarecrows out of buffalo hide. The Mandan women also performed daily cleansing rituals before entering their gardens by rubbing sage over their bodies. They believed this would protect their crops from worms and disease.

Harvesting began in late August with squash and ended in October with corn. After harvest, women would dry the corn in scaffolds built above the ground. After the corn was dry women picked the seeds that they would use for the next year's crops, and the rest was buried with other dried garden items in underground storage pits to preserve them through the winter. These garrets took days to build and were deep enough to require a ladder to enter. When finished they were lined with grass and buffalo hide. The dried vegetables and seeds were placed inside. The garrets were then covered with a layer of buffalo hide, a layer of dirt, and then grass on top. In comparison to the traditions of the other native tribes, these techniques impressed white traders and scouts as uncharacteristically advanced.

But the most mysterious of the Mandan characteristics was their physical appearance. Unlike other natives encountered by early explorers, the Mandan were purported to have mixed complexion that varied from white to almost white, blue and green eyes, and reddish or blondish hair color. All these characteristics suggest European genetics were at some point introduced to tribal bloodlines.

Some theories name Paul Knutson, a thirteenth-century Norwegian, as a possible candidate for having introduced a Nordic/European genetic strain and Christian cultural nuances to the American Midwest. This theory arose because the Mandan built their settlements using an architectural style unknown anywhere else in North America but common in medieval Norway.

In a letter dated January 22, 1804, to Meriwether Lewis, President Jefferson specifically requests the expedition to make contact with and verify rumors of the existence of a white, blue-eyed tribe of natives that had come to be referred to as the "Welsh Indians" because of the similarities between the language of the Mandans and the language of the Welsh. The original source of these claims cannot be pinpointed with exact accuracy, but they had circulated enough that the issue became a matter of great importance to government officials. Documented accounts begin in 1738, when Pierre Gaultier de Varennes, Sieur de la Vérendrye, took an expedition from his forts in present-day Manitoba to what is now North Dakota in search of this mysterious tribe.

During this expedition, near the banks of the Missouri River, de Vérendrye found a stone cairn with a small stone tablet inscribed on both sides with unfamiliar characters. Jesuit scholars in Quebec later described the writing on the stone as Tartarian—a runic script similar to Norse runes. Professor Peter Kalm of the Swedish Royal Academy of Sciences interviewed Captain de Vérendrye about this discovery in Quebec. The tablet was reportedly shipped to France, stored with other archaeological artifacts in a church at Rouen, and buried under tons of rubble by a direct bomb hit during World War II.

Vérendrye located the Mandan village in what is now MacLean County, North Dakota, between Minot and Bismarck. It was a large and well-fortified town with 130 houses laid out in streets. The fort's palisades and ramparts were not unlike European battlements, with a dry moat around the perimeter. More remarkable, Vérendrye noted many of the Mandan had light skin, fair hair, and "European" features. Vérendrye described their houses as "large and spacious," very clean, with separate rooms.

On August 24, 1784, the *Pennsylvania Packet and Daily Advertiser* reported that "a new nation of white people" had been discovered about two thousand miles to the west of the Appalachians, "acquainted with the principles of the Christian religion" and "extremely courteous and civilized." The rumor spread, and somewhere along the line a possible connection of Welsh ancestry was suggested.

In 1796 Welsh explorer John Evans set out to search for the Mandan, hoping to find proof that their language contained Welsh words. Evans spent the winter of 1796–97 with a tribe of Mandan but found no evidence of any Welsh influence. In July 1797 Evans wrote a letter to a Dr. Samuel Jones that said, "Thus having explored and charted the Missurie for 1,800 miles and by my Communications with the Indians this side of the Pacific Ocean from 35 to 49 degrees of Latitude, I am able to inform you that there is no such People as the Welsh Indians."

Evans's conclusion was directly contradicted by Lewis and Clark in 1804 and again in 1832 by George Catlin, a lawyer, frontiersman, and pictorial historian who spent several months living among the Mandan.

It was through Catlin's accounts and art that it was proved beyond what many could doubt that the Mandan indeed were a race descending from European ancestry. Some speculate that Evans may not have reached an actual Mandan settlement, claiming that the evidence provided by Catlin is indisputable.

When the Corps of Discovery entered the world of the Mandan in October 1804, the tribal leaders were receptive to the goals of the expedition. Lewis and Clark found the Mandan people to be extremely hospitable, and the Corps of Discovery prepared to winter on the Missouri River, building a log fort made of cottonwood tree trunks. The men in the expedition cut the lumber from the riverbanks, building a triangular fort facing the river just downstream from the nearby Mandan and Hidatsa villages. They called it Fort Mandan.

For the next five months the fort was a beehive of activity as the expedition made preparations for heading westward to the Pacific Ocean. While there Lewis and Clark interviewed several trappers who could assist as guides and interpreters. It was here that Lewis and Clark hired Toussaint Charbonneau, whose wife, Sacagawea, spoke the Shoshone language. The explorers knew they would need to communicate with the Shoshone tribes as they neared the headwaters of the Missouri River. Sacagawea, who was just fourteen years old, pregnant, and had been long separated from her tribe, would become essential to the success of the expedition. The Corps of Discovery stayed at Fort Mandan until early April, when they set out westward along the Missouri River, but not before documenting over a period of six months important details about the Mandan, their way of life, their sacred beliefs, and their astonishing "almost white" appearance.

With their Hidatsa friends and neighbors the Mandan lay at the center of trade along the upper Missouri River, inhabiting what is now central North Dakota. At the time of Lewis and Clark's arrival, they lived in two villages, Matootonha and Rooptahee. Matootonha was located on the western bank of the Missouri, and Rooptahee was directly north, on the river's eastern bank. The Corps of Discovery built Fort Mandan across the river from Matootonha.

In contrast to the relations of the corps with the aggressive Arikaras of the region, the corps and the Mandan were friendly throughout the duration of the expedition's stay. The Mandan supplied the Americans with food throughout the winter at their newly constructed home, Fort Mandan, in exchange for a steady stream of trade goods. When food became scarce, members of the corps accompanied the Mandan on a buffalo hunt. Sheheke (Bigwhite) and Black Cat, chiefs from Matootonha and Roohaptee, met often with Lewis and Clark, and the corps participated in many of the Mandan ceremonial rituals. Lewis and Clark hoped to establish peace between the Mandan and the nearby Arikaras. In spite of arranging peace talks between the two tribes, conflict broke out again as winter approached.

Of their experience living among the Mandan, William Clark wrote this in his journal: "I set myself down with the bigwhite man Chiefe [Mandan Chief Bigwhite (Sheheke)] and made a number of enquiries into the tradition of his nation. . . . He told me his nation first came out of the ground . . . and saw Buffalow and every kind of animal also grapes, plumbs, c . . . and determined to go up and live upon earth, and great numbers . . . got upon earth, men womin and children."[4]

In his investigation regarding the origins of the mysterious Mandan, Clark was told of the former's belief in a future state after death, a belief that is also connected with the theory of their origin. The Mandan legend describes a whole nation that lived in one large village, underground, near a subterranean lake. A grapevine extended its roots down to their habitation and gave them a view of the light. Some of the more adventurous climbed up the vine, and were delighted with the sight of the earth, which they found covered with buffalo and rich with every kind of fruit.

They returned with the grapes they had gathered, and their countrymen were so pleased with the grapes' taste that the whole nation resolved to leave their dull residence for the charms of the upper region. Men, women, and children ascended by means of the vine, but, when about half the nation had reached the surface of the earth, a corpulent woman who was clambering up the vine broke it with her weight, closing off from herself and the rest of the nation the light of the sun. When the Mandan died they expected to return to the original seats of their forefathers, the good reaching the ancient village by means of the lake, which the burden of the sins of the wicked would not enable them to cross.

This peculiar tradition can be interpreted to mean that the present nation at one time in the distant past lived in a large settlement underground, that is, beyond the land, in the sea, the sea being represented by "the subterranean lake." The description of a vine that was used for people to reach the land of the "sun" and gather fruits and so on indicates the free movement of people back and forth between the North American continent and this other place the Mandan refer to as the "large village." In the new continent the land was filled with buffalo and all kinds of fruits, and the land was colonized, or settled. Perhaps the building traditions from the original "large village" were also acquired, and there were actual cities with streets built in the new continent. And then something happened that cut these people off. Contact was not established again. Whatever happened that severed contact between the two lands was of catastrophic proportion.

During the 1860s Major James W. Lynd lived among the Dakotas and wrote a book about them before meeting a violent death at their hands. Lynd supports the aforementioned explanation with the fact that the legends of the Iowa natives, who were a branch of the Dakotas and relatives of the Mandan, relate that at one point in antiquity all the different tribes were originally one, and they all lived together on an island, or at least across a large body of water toward the east, or the sunrise. According to these legends they crossed this body of water in skin canoes, but they did not know how long the crossing took, or whether the water was salt or fresh.

These legends speak of "huge skiffs, in which their ancestors of long ago floated for weeks, finally gaining dry land." This account is certainly a reference to ships and long sea voyages. The ceremonies further tell a story that "the world was once a great tortoise, borne on the waters, and covered with earth, and that when one day, in digging the soil, a tribe of white men, who had made holes in the earth to a great depth digging for badgers, at length pierced the shell of the tortoise, it sank, and the water covering it drowned all men with the exception of one, who saved himself in a boat; and when the earth re-emerged, sent out a dove, who returned with a branch of willow in its beak."[5]

Twenty-six years after the departure of the Corps of Discovery, George Catlin went in search of the Mandan, locating them and living among them for eight years. Before setting off on his journey Catlin met with then Governor William Clark, who told Catlin he would find the Mandan to be "a strange people and half-white." Catlin describes the tribe as possessing strange hair colors and strange eye colors such as blue and hazel. He speculated at the time that the Mandan had descended from Celts, and that their appearance and atypical customs were perhaps the result of generations of intermarrying and breeding with Welsh explorers and their descendants. Later visitors noted that the languages of the Mandan and Welsh were so similar that the Mandan showed clear comprehension when spoken to in Welsh. Catlin described Mandan women as possessing strikingly Northern European features and found the Mandan in general to be "a very interesting and pleasing people in their personal appearance and manners, differing in many respects, both in looks and customs, from all the other tribes I have seen."[6]

The more time he spent with the Mandan, the more curious Catlin considered them to be. He discovered, for example, that the Mandan claimed to be descended from a white man who arrived in a giant canoe after a flood had destroyed the earth. Oral tradition tells that his vessel became perched on a mountaintop and that a dove was sent out to seek land. It returned with a willow branch in its beak. Similarities to the biblical account of Noah are hard to deny.

An additional detail that adds veracity to the tales of the curious Mandan can be found in a statement made by then Governor William Clark to Catlin prior to his departure in search of the Mandan. Catlin mentions this during his general descriptions of his experience with the legendary tribe:

> Their traditions, so far as I have learned them, afford us no informa-
> tion of their having had any knowledge of white men before the visit
> of Lewis and Clark. Since that time there have been but very few
> visits from white men to the place, and surely not enough to have
> changed the complexions and the customs of a nation. And I recol-
> lect perfectly well that Governor [William] Clark told me before I
> started for this place, that I would find the Mandan a strange people
> and half-white. So forcibly have I been struck with the peculiar ease
> and elegance of these people, together with their diversity of com-
> plexions, the various colours of their hair and eyes; the singularity of
> their language, and their peculiar and unaccountable customs, that
> I am fully convinced that they have sprung from some other origin
> than that of the other North American Tribes, or that they are an
> amalgam of natives with some civilized race.[7]

George Catlin was familiar with at least some of the Madoc stories, "which," as he put it, "I will suppose everybody has read, rather than quote them at this time." The Mandan, according to Catlin, "might pos-sibly be the remains of this lost colony, amalgamated with a tribe, or part of a tribe, of the natives, which would account for the unusual appear-ances of this tribe of Indians, and also for the changed character and customs of the Welsh colonists, provided this be the remains of them."[8]

During the years he lived with the Mandan, Catlin traced their old village sites down the Missouri and to the mouth of the Ohio River. During these explorations he found remains of fortified towns, some enclosing "a great many acres."

There are many flood references in the Mandan legends and those of other tribes. Even more intriguing is that in the center of the religious ceremonies of the Mandan, we find that they kept an image of an ark, preserved from generation to generation, and performed ceremonies that refer plainly to the destruction of a land and to the arrival of one who survived the flood and brought to this new land the news of the catastrophic destruction. Catlin gives us a bird's-eye view of this unique ceremony, which is no longer being danced.

In the centre of the village is an open space, or public square, 150 feet in diameter and circular in form, which is used for all public games and festivals, shows and exhibitions. The lodges around this open space front in, with their doors toward the centre; and in the middle of this stands an object of great religious veneration, on account of the importance it has in connection with the annual religious ceremonies. This object is in the form of a large hogshead, some eight or ten feet high, made of planks and hoops, containing within it some of their choicest mysteries or medicines. They call it the "Big Canoe." On the day set apart for the commencement of the ceremonies a solitary figure is seen approaching the village. During the deafening din and confusion within the pickets of the village the figure discovered on the prairie continued to approach with a dignified step, and in a right line toward the village; all eyes were upon him, and he at length made his appearance within the pickets, and proceeded toward the centre of the village, where all the chiefs and braves stood ready to receive him, which they did in a cordial manner by shaking hands, recognizing him as an old acquaintance, and pronouncing his name, Nu-mohk-muck-a-nah (the first or only man). The body of this strange personage, which was chiefly naked, was painted with white clay, so as to resemble at a distance a white man. He enters the medicine lodge, and goes through certain mysterious ceremonies. During the whole of this day Nu-mohk-muck-a-nah (the first or only man) travelled through the village, stopping in front of each man's lodge, and crying until the owner of the lodge came out and asked who he was, and what was the matter? To which he replied by narrating the sad catastrophe which had happened on the earth's surface by the overflowing of the waters, saying that "he was the only person saved from the universal calamity"; that he landed his big canoe on a high mountain in the west, where he now resides; that he has come to open the medicine lodge, which must needs receive a present of an edged tool from the owner of every wigwam, that it may be sacrificed to the water; for, he says, "if this is not done there will be another flood, and no one will be saved, as it was with such tools that the big canoe was made." Having visited every lodge in the village during the day, and having received such a present from each as a hatchet, a knife, etc. (which is undoubtedly always prepared ready for the occasion), he places them in the medicine lodge; and, on the last day of the ceremony, they are thrown into a deep place in the river—"sacrificed to the Spirit of the Waters."[9]

Describing the dance performed by twelve men around the ark, Catlin says: "They arrange themselves according to the four cardinal points; two are painted perfectly black, two are vermilion color, some were painted partially white. They dance a dance called 'Bel-lohck-na-pie,'" with horns on their heads, like those used in Europe as symbolic of Baal. "It would seem," wrote George Catlin, "that these people must have had some proximity to some part of the civilized world; or that missionaries or others have been formerly among them, inculcating the Christian religion and the Mosaic account of the Flood."[10]

It is a well-known fact that in the various philosophies and religions throughout the world, we find traces or mention of the flood. The Mandan legend describes the earth as a large tortoise. It moves slowly and carries a great deal of earth on its back. Long ago there was a nation of people who are now dead because their land sank into the water. All the people were drowned except for one man. Neither the Mandan nor Catlin had heard of Atlantis, making this account all the more intriguing.

In 1838 a steamboat belonging to the American Fur Company carried up the Missouri the end of the Mandans. A deadly wave of smallpox broke out from the infected crew during a stop at one of the Mandan villages. The tribe didn't stand a chance. Those who weren't killed immediately by the disease decided to take their own lives. During the next two months, the Mandan were decimated to near extinction. Adding insult to injury, the survivors were made slaves by their bitter enemies, the Sioux and Arikara.

Nearly thirty years later all the tribes were swindled out of most of their land and set up on reservations. In 1870 the remaining North Dakota tribes were huddled together and thrown onto a new reservation. Renamed the Three Affiliated Tribes, the surviving Arikaras, Mandans, and Hidatsa were now mere shells of their former selves, less concerned with their ancient heritage and more interested in alcohol. The *Condensed American Cyclopedia* reported in 1877 that the Mandans "are now with the Riccarees (Arikaras) and Gros Ventres (Hidatsa) at Fort Berthold, Dakota. . . . They live partly by agriculture. They are lighter in complexion than most tribes."

The last full-blooded Mandan passed away in 1973, ending the history of these mysterious people, whom George Catlin praised: "A better, more honest, hospitable and kind people, as a community, are not to be found in the world. No set of men that ever I associated with have better hearts than the Mandans, and none are quicker to embrace and welcome a white man than they are—none will press him closer to his bosom, that the pulsation of his heart may be felt, than a Mandan; and no man in any country will keep his word and guard his honour more closely."[11]

Whether the Mandan descended from Scandinavians, or Madoc's Welshmen, or Atlanteans we will never know. Lewis and Clark were in awe of the likeness in the Mandan legends to the biblical story of the flood. They also knew the Mandan were white, because blue eyes and blond-brunette hair are indisputable European features. These remarkable people have left in their wake a mystery that may never be solved.

Six

Voyagers of the Pacific Coast and the Kennewick Man

After a cold and confounding winter with the Mandans, the Corps of Discovery were ready to step once again into the great unknown. The mighty Pacific Ocean and the untamed West were waiting for them. But deep in their guts they knew, somehow, this had all been explored before.

In continuing their journey the Corps of Discovery sent their keelboat back down the Missouri River with a few men and items that had been gathered and sorted for President Jefferson. These included an updated report of the expedition, soil samples, minerals, plants, rudimentary tools and items gathered from the natives, live birds, and a prairie dog, which had never been heard of in the East. Considering the travelers ate some two hundred prairie dogs during the expedition, one wonders if President Jefferson prepared a meal with this one as well.

The rest of the expedition, including Sacagawea, her husband, and their newborn baby, Jean Baptiste, continued their way west up the river in the smaller pirogues. Waterfalls and fierce rapids were progressively making the river impassable. As they made their way into present-day Montana the captains encountered an abundance of wildlife, including buffalo, bighorn sheep, wolves, and a new threat to their survival. The Mandan had warned Lewis and Clark of a creature of such size and strength that it would take many warriors to bring it down. This terrifying new enemy was the grizzly bear.

The expedition would learn to avoid and respect these feared beasts. Lewis was even chased within inches of his life after shooting one. Luckily the bleeding bear gave up the chase after Lewis jumped into a river. Of the grizzly bear Lewis writes, "This bear being so hard to die rather intimidates us all; I must confess that I do not like the gentlemen and had rather fight two Indians than one bear; there is no other chance to conquer them by a single shot but by shooting them through the brains. . . . The fleece and skin were as much as two men could possibly carry."[1]

During the corps' travels, Sacagawea became an important intermediary between the adventurers and the native tribes they encountered. Her presence soothed many of these tribal members, as it was known that warring tribes generally didn't travel with women. Sacagawea translated between various tribes with the help of her husband, the French Canadian trapper Charbonneau, who would relay messages to Rene Jessaume or Frances Labiche. Jessaume and Labiche, in turn, would translate messages into English for the party leaders. Sacagawea also helped forage for edible and medicinal plants, roots, and berries. At one point during the journey Sacagawea saved important supplies and Lewis's journals from washing overboard as the expedition negotiated a storm on the Missouri River.

On August 13, 1805, Lewis and several companions saw a group of two Shoshone women and a male scout. Lewis greeted them and gave the women gifts he had brought with him. The group was brought to a Shoshone village under the leadership of a man named Cameahwait, whom Sacagawea recognized as her own brother. This improbable event proved to be extremely fortunate for Lewis and Clark. They of course included Sacagawea in all their dealings with the Shoshone leader.

On August 17 the tight group of negotiators sealed a pact of mutual friendship and support, and Chief Cameahwait agreed to sell the Corps of Discovery all the horses that they needed for the rest of the journey.

Although Sacagawea had been reunited with her family, she chose to continue with the expedition. In September 1805, when the Corps of Discovery encountered the Salish tribe, the latter feared for their lives at the hands of white warriors, and it was Sacagawea's presence that calmed their worries, proving again how indispensable she was in establishing relations with the natives. The Salish agreed to sell supplies and horses for the expedition and welcomed the Americans and their Shoshone guide into their community. What we know today of Sacagawea's involvement in the expedition comes from the personal diaries of Lewis and Clark. The helpful girl comes alive through the eyes of these two American men. And though the mission to open up the West had fallen upon them, Sacagawea's immeasurable contribution cannot be dismissed.

In early August 1805, Lewis and three other members of the Corps of Discovery headed toward Beaverhead Rock in search of inhabitants. They reached Lemhi Pass, a two-mile stretch across the Montana-Idaho border, on August 12, 1805. Lemhi Pass bridges the gap between the ranges of the Rockies. The crossing of this pass—the Continental Divide—became one of the most important achievements of Lewis and Clark's expedition. They were the first Americans to venture by land into a territory being disputed by other countries.

By finding and mapping a land route to the Pacific Ocean, Lewis and Clark were fulfilling the key priority of the mission and bringing the Pacific Northwest into the history of the United States. In his journal that day Lewis wrote:

> the road took us to the most distant fountain of the waters of the Mighty Missouri in surch of which we have spent so many toilsome days and wristless nights. thus far I had accomplished one of those great objects on which my mind has been unalterably fixed for many years, judge then of the pleasure I felt in all[a]ying my thirst with this pure and ice-cold water here I halted a few minutes and rested myself. two miles below McNeal had exultingly stood with a foot

on each side of this rivulet and thanked his god that he had lived to bestride the mighty & heretofore deemed endless Missouri. after refreshing ourselves we proceeded on to the top of the dividing ridge from which I discovered immence ranges of high mountains still to the West of us with their tops partially covered with snow. . . . here I first tasted the water of the great Columbia river.[2]

It is hard to imagine what went through Lewis's mind while he stood looking at the Rocky Mountains to the east, with range upon range of rugged mountains and peaks fading in the west. This view told Lewis that it would be a long time before he and the Corps of Discovery reached the shores of the Pacific Ocean. For the next two hundred miles the expedition struggled with rain, snow, and near starvation as they made their way into the Bitterroot Mountains. There they suffered frostbite, hunger, and dehydration. Lewis and Clark seemed to lose some of the enthusiasm that had carried them thus far, as evidenced by one of Clark's journal entries: "I have been wet and as cold in every part as I ever was in my life, indeed I was at one time fearfull my feet would freeze in the thin Mockirsons which I wore."[3]

The next day Lewis made the following grim entry: "I directed the horses to be gotten up early being determined to force my march as much as the abilities of our horses would permit. this morning we finished the remainder of our last coult. we dined & suped on a skant proportion of portable soupe . . ."[4]

Atop the 7,000-foot-tall ridge they found no water. Their meal consisted of a soup made from melted snow and the leftovers of a young colt. After traveling for more than a month through dangerous high mountains and heavily forested hills, with little rest along the way, the expedition finally came out of the Bitterroot Mountains.

On September 20, 1805, the Corps of Discovery encountered the natives that came to be known as the Nez Percé. The French name Nez Percé, which means "pierced nose," is a name mistakenly ascribed to the tribe by a Corps of Discovery interpreter who confused them with the

Chinook Tribe, whose members did display piercing and shared fishing and trading sites with the Nez Percé tribe. Today the most common self-designation used by the Nez Percé tribe is Niimiipu.

The first contact was between what must have appeared as an odd-looking stranger with white skin and red hair, William Clark, and three scared native boys. The Nez Percé had never seen a white man before, and they graciously welcomed the exhausted Corps of Discovery to their camp at Weippe Prairie.

The great Chief Joseph spoke highly of the strange folk that arrived from the mountains, saying:

> The first white men of your people who came to our country were named Lewis and Clark. They brought many things that our people had never seen. They talked straight and our people gave them a great feast as proof that their hearts were friendly. They made presents to our chiefs and our people made presents to them. We had a great many horses of which we gave them what they needed, and they gave us guns and tobacco in return. All the Nez Percé made friends with Lewis and Clark and agreed to let them pass through their country and never to make war on white men. This promise the Nez Percé have never broken.[5]

These noble words weighed true until the discovery of gold on the chief's land.

Lewis and Clark were intrigued with the Nez Percé for many reasons, not the least of which were their beautiful and unusual horses, the Appaloosa, a highly refined breed. It was exclusive to their tribe, even though neighboring tribes coveted it. When Lewis saw the Appaloosa, he compared them to some of the more elegant horses of Europe.

The Nez Percé had mastered the art of breeding—unknown to other tribes—such as mating the best stallion with the best mare and practicing castration of lesser stallions. (All the other tribes caught wild horses or stole them from each other.) It is generally believed that horses were brought to the New World by the Spanish around 1780 and that the plains Native Americans acquired them soon after that. Yet even if the Spanish breeds had been rushed to the Pacific Northwest as soon as they came off the Spanish galleons, the time span from 1780 would have been insufficient to achieve the specific genetic developments present when Lewis and Clark first saw the horses in September 1805.

Thus it is that we must question how a native tribe in the northwest corner of a land divided by almost insurmountable physical boundaries could possess such a defined breed. The few schoolbooks that actually mention the subject suggest that the Appaloosa is a mixture of Asian and Spanish breeds and that the Northwest natives obtained these Spanish breeds from the tribes of the South. However, most books omit to mention where the Asian breeds may have come from, leaving it to be assumed Asian horses also crossed the Bering Strait.

Further investigation leads us to believe the Appaloosa bred by the Nez Percé were Chinese, and there was evidence at the time of the Lewis and Clark expedition to substantiate this claim. In addition there exists strong proof that the Pacific Northwest had contact with Chinese civilizations by water, and not only by the trickle suggested across the Bering land bridge. Over the years this evidence has been coyly yet ruthlessly covered, altered, or outright destroyed.

The Appaloosa appears in pictographs of ancient Asian and Chinese art. The Nez Percé horses were known for their speed, endurance, and surefootedness. The Appaloosa in particular were short legged and stocky, with large heads and thick necks. Their spotted rumps are their defining characteristic. In the second century BCE, Chinese emperor Wu Ti imported Arabian horses into China to improve their mediocre native stock. Among this new influx were the spotted horses. Evidence of spotted horses has been common in China for the past two thousand years as documented in surviving art.

After they had been fed and were sufficiently rested, the Corps of Discovery were ready to resume their journey. The generous Nez Percé people gave them supplies and information about river routes to the Pacific Ocean. The explorers left their horses in the trust of the Nez Percé until their return.

It is interesting to note that in this beautiful valley where the Nez Percé lived freely, there is a mound so large it looks like a hill. According to local legend this mound is supposed to contain deep within it the heart of a great monster killed during the beginning of the world. There is no mention of this hill or its intriguing mythology in any of the journals of the men from the expedition despite very clear instructions from President Jefferson for soil samples and the like. Did Lewis and Clark see the mound? How is it possible they could have missed it?

Within a few days after leaving the Nez Percé, Lewis and Clark reached the Clearwater River, a tributary of the Snake River, which led to the Columbia. The two rivers converge in the general area near Kennewick, Washington. On October 16, 1805, when they reached the Narrows of the Columbia, Lewis saw the water "boiling and whirling in every direction" over jagged rocks. They flung their canoes safely through the obstacles and found themselves on the waters of the Columbia, rushing toward the Pacific Ocean.

The expedition was traversing a particularly awe-inspiring territory, rich in anthropological treasures, when Clark wrote in his journal:

> in those narrows the water was agitated in a most Shocking manner boils Swell and whorl pools, we passed with great risque It being impossible to make a portage of the Canoes, about 2 miles lower passed a verry bad place between 2 rocks one large and in the middle of the river here our Canoes took in some water, I put all the men who Could not Swim on Shore; and sent a fiew articles Such as guns & papers, and landed at a village of 20 houses on the Stard. Side in a Deep bason where the river apprd. to be blocked up with emence rocks.[6]

It is important to mention here the intriguing area that surrounded the Corps of Discovery during these last maneuvers that would bring them within view of the Pacific. The region described by Lewis and Clark no longer resembles the landscape described in Clark's journal. The area had long been a gathering place for people from the Warm Springs, Yakama, Umatilla, Nez Percé, and other tribes. Some, like the Wishram, Cloud, and Lishkam tribes, lived there permanently and fished with nets and spears between The Dalles and Celilo Falls.

Other natives visited seasonally to practice their religion and take the opportunity to trade and socialize. Others came to harvest spawning salmon. The number of Native American villages in the area was greater than any other Lewis and Clark had encountered in their journey. Because they were abundant, salmon was the currency that supported the tribal economy. Today salmon have been reduced to a meager number that represents less than 1 percent of the numbers observed by early explorers. For centuries this area near the river was a sort of campground, or communal gathering center, where religious ceremonies, including burials, took place. Annual ceremonies that brought together thousands would logically make this place the largest burial ground of natives in the area. Indeed it was.

Lewis and Clark arrived in the area of Horsethief Butte on October 24, 1805. Because of the rough weather and harsh terrain they didn't do much exploring.

Later some of the oldest pictographs in North America were found in this area. Discoveries included sacred petroglyphs—drawings chipped or ground into rock—that depict tribal legends, hunting scenes, what appear to be alien beings, and mystical imagery. This is evidence of the extreme age of the gatherings that took place in the area. Celilo Falls now only exists in the imagination; it has been reduced to a lake. Sitting behind The Dalles Dam since 1957, this reservoir eliminated important fishing grounds for many native tribes. For more than ten thousand years Native Americans lived and fished in the Celilo Falls area. But today their ghosts remain silent and show no proof of the proud, ancient heritage that once existed in the area.

The seeming erasure of history has much to do with the fact that the U.S. Army Corps of Engineers owns this part of the Columbia River. In 1957 the corps specifically chose the area of Celilo Falls to build a dam, where hundreds of historical petroglyphs and perhaps more artifacts that would provide proof of an ancient, technological civilization were to be found. Rising waters caused by the dam flooded the Celilo area, including the falls, burying forever the ancient petroglyphs, along with the ancient history of the Columbia Basin. Only forty-three of the ancient rock symbols were chosen to be moved to a new location.

You can visit these remaining glyphs at Washington's Columbia Hills State Park, about an hour and a half away from their original location. According to the U.S. Army Corps of Engineers, this is "the best place to see native petroglyphs in the Northwest"—unless one has gills, in which case one can see the hundreds that are under water.

By early November the Corps of Discovery had overcome the Cascades, and the last mountain obstacle was behind them. They were now moving through tidewater by the White Salmon River junction, which they called Canoe Creek because of a cluster of canoes seen at the river's mouth when they drifted by. There isn't much noted about this area, which is intriguing. Did they stop? Were they more impressed by the view of Mount Hood to the south?

Lewis, Clark, and the men of the Corps of Discovery were the first white Americans to see Mount Hood. White Salmon River runs through what was once a giant lava tube that collapsed on itself. The vegetation on the area's riverbank is a strange mix of oak trees, cottonwoods, and ponderosas, with Douglas fir, maidenhair ferns, western red cedar, and Pacific yew, vastly different from the desertlike terrain they had just passed through days before. One can only imagine the awe with which the explorers must have viewed this uncharted territory. Without a clear notion of how, or if, they would return home, Lewis and Clark, the young Sacagawea, and the Corps of Discovery risked mountains, falls, and rapids that today would intimidate the most skilled sportsmen.

Rather than die, as the native spectators along the shore expected them to, they lived to tell a tale that continues to enthrall.

On November 7, 1805, Clark famously wrote in his journal: "Ocian in view! O, the joy!" when he incorrectly thought he was within a short distance from the great Pacific. And then on the morning of November 8, 1805, Clark wrote that the entire party changed clothes. A custom of that time was for travelers to stop at the end of a long journey and ready themselves by putting on their best clothes for arrival. This indicates that Lewis and Clark were expecting November 8 to be the day they would stand on the shores of the Pacific Ocean. With only twenty miles to go, the weather changed dramatically, and they were forced to hang on for dear life. They were hit by rolling breakers so big they had to turn around. This brave group that had pushed ahead against all odds was now facing a river entrance that in later years would be known as the Graveyard of Ships.

After two other attempts that day they were forced to camp on a little beach. During the night they experienced thunderstorms, wind, hail, rocks falling from the cliffs above them, and huge logs tossed to the shore by the pounding surf. They abandoned most of their supplies, buried their canoes, and found shelter in a wooded area around the point. When the weather finally changed days later, and they were able to leave their refuge behind, Clark referred to the place as "this dismal nitch."

Historian Rex Ziak's *In Full View,* written in 2001, is a beautifully designed tome that chronicles each step of the expedition carefully and accurately thanks to a mislabeled map drawn by Clark. Ziak explains it was a virtual treasure map with coordinates pointing to a spot called Station Camp. It was here, late on November 15, 1805, that, according to Ziak's carefully reconstructed account, the Corps of Discovery was finally able to establish a stable camp, and where Clark would write words of great significance: "This I could plainly See would be the extent of our journey by water . . . in full view of the Ocian." This is further substantiated by the entry made by Sgt. Patrick Gass in his diary the next day, November 16, 1805: "We are now at the end of our voyage which has been completely accomplished."

According to Ziak, this entry means Station Camp was where Lewis and Clark's voyage of discovery was completed—Station Camp in Washington, not Fort Clatsop in Oregon. Ziak further reinforces this conclusion by noting in his journal that within days of arriving, the explorers were ready to head home. The weather on November 24 caused them to reconsider their departure plans, and it was on the evening of that day that the two captains polled the entire party about whether to spend the winter near the ocean on the south side of the Columbia or somewhere farther upriver. This now famous "vote" was the first in American history to include a black slave (York, Clark's servant) and an Indian woman. The vote took place at Station Camp. While the famous vote for a winter camp was being discussed, Clark would carve on a tree: "William Clark, by land from the U. States in 1804 and 1805." It was in this peninsula on the southwestern tip of Washington where Meriwether Lewis and William Clark ended their trip west.

It was now a matter of waiting out three-and-a-half harsh winter months at Fort Clatsop, in present-day Oregon, before beginning the long journey back home.

During the long winter it became apparent that the worlds of Lewis and Clark and that of the natives were as different as night and day. The explorers came from a land of scientific development, whereas the tribes had beliefs and customs deeply rooted in legend. The natives took their names from sacred animals and places. They explained the forces of the universe with fables and myths.

When Lewis and Clark finally reached the Pacific Ocean, they literally became beachcombers, traveling as far south as the area now called Ecola Beach State Park and as far north as Astoria, Oregon. During their exploration of the area, William Clark would give Tillamook Head, located between Seaside and Cannon Beach, the title of "the Steepest worst and highest mountain I ever ascended."

Shortly after December 25 in 1806, Clark and twelve other expedition members, including Sacagawea, climbed over rocky hills, fighting their way through thick bushes and trees. From this vantage point the members of the climbing party saw the skeleton of a beached whale south of what is now Ecola State Park.

Perhaps a little more exploring in this area and they might have unearthed ancient Chinese coins. In an article written in 2006, journalist Richard Blake interestingly mentions ancient Chinese coins from the Sung Dynasty that had been found at the mouth of the Ecola River. These coins are kept at the Cannon Beach Historical Society museum in Cannon Beach. In addition, records kept by the Sung Dynasty claim that Chinese explorers reached the West Coast possibly seventy years before Columbus reached the East Coast.

The amount of anthropological and archaeological oddities that connect the Washington and Oregon coasts with Asia, and specifically China, are scarce. But they do exist. The problem remains that most of the evidence has gone into private collections. The little that remains at universities is ignored and tucked away in dusty archives. Some examples of anomalies that have come to light are the documenting of various native groups on Vancouver Island who look distinctly Chinese compared to their neighboring natives. In addition, cave burials along the west coast of Vancouver Island have turned up distinctly Chinese relics, including skeletons. These skeletons are different in size and stature from those of native peoples along the coast. Excavations in Tilamook County by the University of Oregon in the early 1970s unearthed ancient Chinese vases and pottery.

In the early to mid 1970s, Washington State University archaeologists examined a piece of bronzework that was hauled up by a fishing boat near the mouth of the Strait of Juan de Fuca. The archaeologists, led by Dr. Richard D. Daugherty of WSU, thought the piece to be of Chinese origin and possibly a ship's decoration of some kind. Daugherty had hoped the university would acquire the relic, but it was sold to a private party and never seen again.

★ ★ ★

The most alluring of all the Asian Pacific Northwest connections is the enigmatic and controversial Kennewick Man. Kennewick Man is the name given to the remains of a prehistoric man found on a bank of the Columbia River near Kennewick, Washington, on July 28, 1996. While swimming in the river during the annual hydroplane races, two college students accidentally made the discovery of a man's skull. It turned out to belong to the most complete ancient skeleton ever found. The bones were dubbed the "Kennewick Man."

Immediately the remains became embroiled in debates about the relationship between Native American religious rights and archaeology that launched a nine-year legal clash between scientists, the federal government, and Native American tribes. The tribes claimed Kennewick Man as their ancestor. The long dispute made the remains an international celebrity, the subject of documentaries, websites, books, and even the cover of *Time* magazine. The controversy became so convoluted that the long litigation process has relegated this amazing cultural discovery to a university basement. Today secrets held by the Kennewick Man continue to be, at least for the public, secret.

Then Benton County Coroner Floyd Johnson reached out to a forensic anthropologist in Richland named Jim Chatters, who studied the bones before a detailed analysis could be made. About a month later Chatters and Johnson announced that the skeleton was about 9,200 years old, and they speculated that the man appeared to be in his forties or fifties when he died, making him very old for that period. Chatters and Johnson noted that the skeleton showed a healed broken arm and a healed broken rib, and they found a roughly 1-inch basalt spear point embedded in the skeleton's pelvic bone (which was not the cause of death). Before a detailed scientific analysis was completed a digital reconstruction of the skull revealed the features were Caucasoid. When the media broke the story, a great deal of coverage emphasized a similarity in appearance between the Kennewick Man and *Star Trek: The*

Next Generation actor Patrick Stewart. This flurry of coverage served the purpose of telling the truth about the discovery of the Kennewick Man, but it depicted the discovery as a joke.

But there is far more to his story.

The history of the colonization of North America by humans has been represented as a trickle of migration across the Bering Strait land bridge during the last Ice Age. More recent archaeological research has begun to uncover an enormous amount of evidence that speaks to the contrary. That evidence suggests that there was a much more complex and sizeable migration to North America. Archaeologists such as Thor Heyerdahl, for example, are convinced that the colonization of North America by humans came in multiple waves, via different means, and from different regions. The Kennewick Man is further evidence of such a colonization wave.

The U.S. Army Corps of Engineers owns the Columbia River shoreline through the Tri-Cities, so it claimed ownership of the skeleton. However, according to the Native American Graves Protection and Repatriation Act (NAGPRA) signed into law by President George H. W. Bush in 1990, if human remains are found on federal lands and their cultural affiliation can be established, the bones must be returned to the affiliated tribe. Based on this act, five Native American nations (the Nez Percé, Umatilla, Yakama, Wannapum, and Colville) claimed the remains as theirs.

In April 1998, to protect any other skeletons and artifacts from the curious hands of archaeologists, the U.S. Army Corps of Engineers covered the Kennewick site with five hundred tons of rock fill.

Curiously, we find the Smithsonian Institution embroiled in the act, with Douglas Owsley, a Smithsonian anthropologist, taking over the disputed remains and refusing to turn them over to any of the native nations. He contends that the remains' potential contributions to science are too great, and that Kennewick Man could not be linked to any one tribe. Owsley, along with eight other anthropologists, filed a lawsuit on the matter in 1996 in U.S. District Court in Portland, Oregon.

The five native nations fought the anthropologists in court, claiming that the repatriation law covered the Kennewick Man and that scientific examinations disrespected Native American beliefs about the sanctity of their dead. In 2002, Judge John Jelderks ruled in the anthropologists' favor. The ruling did not set a timetable for the studies to be completed or published. The Army Corps of Engineers, which remains the legal guardian of Kennewick Man, put him in the Burke Museum, a neutral site agreeable to both the tribes and scientists.

Due to a costly litigation process for the five Native American nations, all but the Umatillas dropped their claims. The Umatilla tribe of Native Americans requested custody of the remains, wanting to bury them according to tribal tradition. However, researchers hoping to study the remains contested their claim. The Umatilla tradition holds that their people have been present on the lands since the dawn of time. The government assertion that Kennewick Man is not Native American is tantamount to the government rejecting their beliefs. Interestingly, the government assertion also lends credence to the argument that Kennewick Man descended from a race other than the indigenous Northwest native peoples.

On February 4, 2004, the U.S. Court of Appeals for the Ninth Circuit ruled that a cultural link between the tribe and the skeleton was not met. The tribe dropped its custody lawsuit, and the ruling supposedly opened the door for more scientific study.

In April 2005, U.S. Senator John McCain introduced and later pushed through an amendment to NAGPRA (Senate Bill 536), which, in section 108, would change the definition of "Native American" from being that which "is indigenous to the United States" to "is or was indigenous to the United States." By that definition Kennewick Man would be Native American, whether or not any link to a contemporary tribe could be found. Proponents of this interpretation argue that this remains in accord with current scientific understanding that it is not in all cases possible for prehistoric remains to be traced to current tribal bloodlines. The difficulty is attributed to a long history of social upheaval, forced resettlement, and extinction of entire ethnicities caused by disease and warfare in the wake of European colonization.

But McCain's redefinition did not remove the controversy surrounding Kennewick Man.

Finally, in July 2005, some of the nation's leading scientists convened in Seattle for ten days to study the remains of the Kennewick Man. After making many detailed measurements, tests, and analyses, they have released some of their findings. But for the public, the secrets of the Kennewick Man are still secret.

C. Loring Brace is a professor of anthropology at the University of Michigan. He was one of the scientists who had to wait nine years to study the famous skeleton.

"One look at that thing, and I knew it was going to relate to the Ainu of Japan," he said. The Ainu were the original and first people of Japan before being hunted into extinction in their homeland. The idea of the Ainu roaming the Northwest represented a radical shift in traditional thinking. When Kennewick Man was first discovered, he was initially thought to be European.

But as Brace explains, "The Ainu don't look like other Japanese. They have light skin, wavy hair and body hair. And their eyes don't look Asian at all."[7]

John Stang, a *Seattle Post-Intelligencer* correspondent who authored a detailed account of Kennewick Man's odyssey, interviewed Brian Irely, a spokesman for the Smithsonian Institution, about when the public may expect to read the conclusions drawn from the examination at the University of Washington's Burke Museum.

Irely replied, "The scientists are unsure how long it will take until their findings are published."[8]

Stephanie Jolivette, the museum's public outreach coordinator, was quoted in the article as saying, "It's odd to me that there hasn't been any preliminary results out."[9]

When the 2006 examination was finished, the only statements offered indicated that the Kennewick Man was likely in his thirties when he died, that the spear wound did not kill him, and that the estimated age of the skeleton was between 8,200 and 9,500 years. They did little more than confirm the original study completed by Chatters and Johnson in 1996.

Since 2006 nothing has been publicly disclosed about the studies conducted on the remains. Today Kennewick Man is stored in boxes in the Burke Museum's basement at a premium of $30,000 a year. The museum does not reveal the remains' exact location for "security reasons," but it is interesting to note that neither the Corps of Engineers nor the Umatilla nation (which had the highest profile during the litigation) have any idea of the progress made by scientists. Nor has either reported seeing the remains of the Kennewick Man since 2006. Other researchers have requested access to the skeleton for their own measurements and DNA studies. But so far the corps has denied every request.

Rather than clearing the area for more revealing investigations, the U.S. Army Corps of Engineers elected to dump five hundred tons of concrete and rock on the discovery site. Rather than make Kennewick Man's remains available to anthropologists or researchers, access is denied. Rather than turning the bones over to the tribe that claims the remains as their ancestor based on legal rights given to them by the government, the bones are kept in a museum basement. Could the answer be that the Kennewick Man is associated with an ancient and advanced civilization and that an explanation as to why his remains have turned up is dreaded by various authorities? Is that why it seems that extreme steps have been taken to patiently remove the discovery from public awareness?

The Kennewick Man can be compared with the discovery of a 10,300-year-old skeleton discovered in On Your Knees Cave on southeast Alaska's Prince of Wales Island. The remains were named Shuka Kaa, which means "Man Ahead of Us." Shuka Kaa was estimated to be roughly twenty years old at the time of his death. The anthropologists involved in this discovery quickly turned the incomplete remains over to the native tribe of the area for burial. Some speculate that a legal battle over incomplete remains that would not likely contribute to current knowledge would be a waste.

Author Michael Cremo's book *Forbidden Archaeology* offers a great deal of additional documentation that suggests modern humankind's antiquity far exceeds accepted chronologies. For example, Cremo offers a report from the June 11, 1891, edition of the *Morrisonville Times*.

A curious find was brought to light by Mrs. S. W. Gulp last Tuesday morning. As she was breaking a lump of coal preparatory to putting it in the scuttle, she discovered, as the lump fell apart, embedded in a circular shape a small gold chain about ten inches in length of antique and quaint workmanship. At first Mrs. Gulp thought the chain had been dropped accidentally in the coal, but as she undertook to lift the chain up, the idea of its having been recently dropped was at once made fallacious, for as the lump of coal broke it separated almost in the middle, and the circular position of the chain placed the two ends near to each other, and as the lump separated, the middle of the chain became loosened while each end remained fastened to the coal.

This is a study for the students of archaeology who love to puzzle their brains over the geological construction of the earth from whose ancient depth the curious is always dropping out. The lump of coal from which this chain was taken is supposed to come from the Taylorville or Pana mines [southern Illinois] and almost hushes one's breath with mystery when it is thought for how many long ages the earth has been forming strata after strata which hid the golden links from view. The chain was an eight-carat gold and weighed eight penny-weights.[10]

He notes that the Illinois State Geological Survey contended that the coal encasing the gold chain was between 260 and 320 million years old.

Another instance involved a report issued in 1871 by William E.

Dubois of the Smithsonian Institution. Dubois reported that several manmade objects were found at unusual depths during drilling in Illinois. The first object was what appeared to be a copper coin. In a letter to the Smithsonian the driller said he discovered the coin stuck to a "common ground auger" after drilling at 125 feet. Later reports suggested that the object had been discovered at a depth of 114 feet rather than 125 feet. The Illinois State Geological Survey offered an estimate for the age of deposits found at the 114-foot level: "sometime between 200,000 and 400,000 years."

Dubois said the coin contained crude inscriptions in a language that he didn't recognize, and that the coin's overall appearance differed from any known coin. Dubois seemed certain that the object was made in a machine shop. He said the uniform thickness of the coin indicated that it had "passed through a rolling-mill; and if the ancient Indians had such a contrivance, it must have been prehistoric."[11]

The object, according to experts noted by Cremo, suggests the existence of a civilization at least two hundred thousand years ago in North America. This directly contradicts the widely held assumption that the earliest humans intelligent enough to make and use coins lived one hundred thousand years ago.

In Whiteside County, Illinois, at a depth of 120 feet, workers discovered a small trove of objects, including "a large copper ring or ferrule, similar to those used on ship spars at the present time. . . . They also found something fashioned like a boat-hook." One observer noted, "There are numerous instances of relics found at lesser depths. A spear-shaped hatchet, made of iron, was found imbedded in clay at 40 feet; and stone pipes and pottery have been unearthed at depths varying from 10 to 50 feet in many localities."[12]

In September 1984 the Illinois State Geological Survey wrote to Cremo and his associates that "the age of deposits at 120 feet in Whiteside County varies greatly. In some places, one would find at 120 feet deposits only 50,000 years old, while in other places one would find Silurian bedrock 410 million years old."[13]

The singular sort of territorial rage evoked by these sorts of claims emerged in 1996 when NBC broadcast a prime-time special called "The Mysterious Origins of Man." The special featured material from Cremo's book, and it sent America's academic and scientific communities into a fit. The reaction from the scientific community was especially fiery, as NBC was inundated with letters from irate scientists. Amid cries of "Hoax!" the scientists tried to force NBC to agree never to reair the broadcast. When that didn't work, opponent scientists took their case to the FCC. In a letter to the FCC, Dr. Allison Palmer, president of the Institute for Cambrian Studies, wrote, "At the very least, NBC should be required to make substantial prime-time apologies to their viewing audience for a sufficient period of time so that the audience clearly gets the message that they were duped."[14]

Wait until they hear about the giants.

Seven

Giants in Ancient America

Meriwether Lewis, described as a giant of American history, may have been preceded by an entire race of real, historical giants.

Despite being a prominent theme in all the world's mythologies, the lore about giants generally remains in the realm of children's tales. It seems odd then that ancient peoples from different parts of the globe would all write and speak of an age of giants.

Genesis 6:4 offers, "There were giants in the earth in those days; and also after that, when the sons of God came in unto the daughters of men, and they bare children to them, the same became mighty men which were of old, men of renown."

In another famous biblical account we learn about the battle between David and Goliath. While digging at Tell es-Safi in 2005, archaeologists from Bar-Ilan University in Israel discovered pottery sherds mentioning the name of Goliath. The writing on the shards represents the oldest Philistine inscriptions ever found. The area of Tell es-Safi was known in ancient times as the lands of Gath; it encompasses an area surrounding two large mounds located on the border between the Judean foothills and the coastal plain. Covering more than a hundred acres, it's one of the most important archaeological sites in Israel. Professor Aren Maeir, director of the Tell es-Safi/Gath Archaeological Project, suggests that the discoveries being made there point to the legends being real.

He says in a press release issued by Bar-Ilan University, "This inscription appears to provide evidence that the biblical story of Goliath is, in fact, based on more or less, the time which is depicted in the biblical text, and recent attempts to claim that Goliath can only be understood in the context of later phases of the Iron Age are unwarranted."[1]

What's more surprising than reified biblical accounts are stories of giants living in the West. Some of the American giants' last days have been preserved in what remains of the writings of the conquistadores. The valuable information contained in the various writings from the Spanish invasion of the New World is so fantastic it's hard to believe what they say.

Thanks to the tremendous amount of research done by Stephen Quayle, who brought to light the verified written accounts of giants from the early sixteenth century, there now appears to be bona fide written evidence that as little as five hundred years ago giants were living in the Americas.

In 1519, Alonzo Álvarez de Pineda mapped the lands along the Gulf Coast, strategically marking the various rivers and bays, noticeable landmarks, and porting areas, all of which belonged to the king of Spain. After covering the coastlines from Florida to as far as Tampico, Mexico, Pineda sailed back to the mouth of the Mississippi River. Pineda was the first Spanish explorer to venture up the mighty Mississippi, and he reports finding a large settlement of native villages inhabited by giants. After the giants proved to be friendly, Pineda and crew settled among them to rest and make repairs.

Pineda detailed the abundance of gold found in the river, and how the natives wore plenty of gold-engraved ornaments. It's amazing how Pineda was more interested in the lands, good food, and the shock of discovering giants than he was in gold. As he sailed back to his home base in Jamaica, he made note of more giants encountered on the various islands of the Texas coast. When Pineda returned, he presented Francisco de Garay, the Spanish governor of Jamaica, with the maps and sketches of the entire Gulf Coast. The first known map of the gulf also included Pineda's writings about the fantastic race of giants living there. These sketches and writings are known as Garay's Cédula and were archived by the famous Spanish compiler Martín Fernández de Navarrete. They can be found today by visiting the Archivo General de Indias, in Seville, Spain.

Twenty years after Pineda mapped the Gulf, Francisco Coronado marched with a huge expedition across the American Southwest searching for the legendary Seven Cities of Cibola, or what we refer to today as El Dorado. While on their quest Coronado's expedition crossed paths with several tribes of Indian giants. We have this information thanks to the writings of Pedro de Castaneda, who accompanied Coronado and wrote the complete and amazing history of the expedition. A fascinating tale concerning giants found in Castaneda's book details the journey made by Hernando de Alarcón.

Low on provisions, a frantic Coronado sent Alarcón to find a river that could bring supplies more easily to the Spanish outposts along the California and Mexican coasts. After nearly destroying his ships and missing the waiting party at the rendezvous point, Alarcón haphazardly floated up the mouth of the murky Colorado River. Alarcón and his men became the first Europeans to fight the rough rapids as he brought his fleet into the heart of the Colorado River, reaching as far as the lower reaches of the Grand Canyon. While coasting up the river, Alarcón and his men came upon a settlement of an estimated two hundred giant warriors. These giants, amazed by foreign intruders on the riverbanks, were ready to attack.

But Alarcón defused the situation by making peace and offering gifts, which eventually won them over. These giants were later categorized with the prevailing tribes of the area as being the Cocopa Indians. A thousand more members of this giant tribe were discovered and reported farther upstream.

Discoveries of giants have also been reported in Mexico. The Dominican friar Diego Durán is responsible for writing some of the earliest Western books on the history and culture of the Aztecs. His family moved from Spain to Mexico City when he was very young, which allowed him to grow up around the remaining natives of Mexico. While attending school he was frequently exposed to Aztec culture, then under the colonial rule of Spain. He continued to study and travel within the remaining city-states of the Aztec empire. In Texcoco he learned to speak and read the native Nahuatl Aztec language. By winning the Aztecs' trust, he was able to gain access to a vast amount of knowledge concerning the history of pre-Columbian Mexico.

His writings are some of the oldest known surviving texts that give us actual firsthand narratives from the ancient Aztecs. Because he spent thirty-two years among the Aztecs gathering information, learning how to read ancient native hieroglyphics, and interviewing old shamans, scholars regard Durán's work as extremely important. In *The History of the Indies of New Spain,* he exhaustively describes the history of Mexico from its mysterious ancient origins up to conquest and occupation by the Spaniards. In these writings the Aztecs were not shy when it came to talking about giants.

But Durán didn't need to hear or read about them. He could see them.

While living in Mexico he came in contact with giant Indians on several occasions. Writing about these encounters, he says emphatically, "It cannot be denied that there have been giants in this country. I can affirm this as an eyewitness, for I have met men of monstrous stature here. I believe that there are many in Mexico who will remember, as I do, a giant Indian who appeared in a procession of the feast of Corpus Christi. He appeared dressed in yellow silk and a halberd at his shoulder and a helmet on his head. And he was all of three feet taller than the others."[2]

Bernal Díaz del Castillo marched as a swordsman in the army under Hernán Cortés during the conquest of Mexico. After surviving these expeditions he lived to be an old man and wrote what is regarded as an exceptionally accurate narrative of the famous campaign. His book would come to be known as *The True History of the Conquest of New Spain.* Unfortunately Díaz died before seeing his book published.

Fifty years later the manuscript was found in a Madrid library. It was finally published in 1632. The book provides an eyewitness account of the conquest of Mexico, and it remains one of the most significant sources documenting the collapse of the Aztec Empire and the Spanish conquest of Mexico. Díaz recounts the history of the now-defeated Tlaxcatec Indians, mentioning a race of enormous giants that had once inhabited their land. During these encounters Díaz even had the chance to examine firsthand evidence of this long-forgotten race.

He writes:

They said their ancestors had told them that very tall men and women with huge bones had once dwelt among them. But because they were a very bad people with wicked customs they had fought against them and killed them, and those of them who remained had died off. And to show us how big these giants had been they brought us the leg-bone of one, which was very thick and the height of an ordinary-sized man, and that was a leg-bone from the hip to the knee. I measured myself against it, and it was as tall as I am, though I am of a reasonable height. They brought other pieces of bone of the same kind, but they were all rotten and eaten away by the soil. We were all astonished by the sight of these bones and felt certain there must have been giants in that land.[3]

An Italian scholar from Venice, Antonio Pigafetta, traveled with famous Portuguese explorer Ferdinand Magellan and his crew on their voyage to the Indies. During the expedition Pigafetta became Magellan's assistant and kept an accurate journal that detailed the various encounters with native giants. In *Magellan's Voyage: A Narrative of the First Circumnavigation*, there are numerous references to giants. Pigafetta amusingly writes:

We had been two whole months in this harbor without sighting anyone when one day (without anyone expecting it) we saw on the shore a huge giant, who was naked, and who danced, leaped and sang, all the while throwing sand and dust on his head. Our Captain ordered one of the crew to walk towards him, telling this man also to dance, leap and sing as a sign of friendship. This he did, and led the giant to a place by the shore where the Captain was waiting. And when the giant saw us, he marveled and was afraid, and pointed to the sky, believing we came from heaven. He was so tall that even the largest of us came only to midway between his waist and his shoulder.[4]

Pigafetta was among the surviving 18 men who returned to Spain in 1522. The other 240 men of the expedition all died, including Magellan.

Around the same time that Magellan was having his difficulties, the famed Italian explorer Amerigo Vespucci was charting the Caribbean islands off the coast of Venezuela. Amerigo, for whom one-third of the world would later be named, wrote about the giants he encountered on the modern-day island of Curaçao.

Recounting this experience, Vespucci writes, "We landed to see if we could find fresh water, and imagining that the island was not inhabited because we saw no people. Going along the shore we beheld very large footprints of men on the sand. And we judged if their other members were of corresponding size, that they must be very big men."[5]

As Vespucci and his men ventured into the island jungle he writes, "We discovered a trail and set ourselves to walk on it two leagues and a half inland; we met with a village of twelve houses in which we did not find anyone except five women, two old ones and three girls so lofty in stature that we gazed at them in astonishment."[6]

Vespucci and his men were invited to eat and drink. While doing so they formed a plan to kidnap the three exotic girls. But their plans dissolved quickly when the giant men of the village returned. In a state of anxiety, Vespucci recalls:

While we were thus plotting, thirty-six men arrived, who entered the house where we were drinking, and they were of such lofty stature that each of them was taller when upon his knees than I was when standing erect. Men that were so well built, it was a famous sight to see them. They were of the stature of giants in their great size and in the proportion of their bodies, which corresponded with their height. When the men entered, some of our fellows were so frightened that at the moment they thought they were done for. The warriors had bows and arrows and tremendous oar blades finished off like swords. When they saw our small stature, they began to converse with us to learn who we were and whence we came. We gave them soft words for the sake of amity and replied to them in sign language that we were men of peace and that we were out to see the world. In fact, we judged it wise to part from them without controversy, and so we went by the same trail by which we had come. They stuck with us all the way to the sea and until we embarked.[7]

Vespucci and company made it safely back to their boats and fired off a few shots from their guns. The frightened giants scattered back into their villages, and Vespucci sailed away. He promptly named Curaçao the Isle of Giants.

One of the most famous and colorful figures of the American Old West was "Buffalo Bill" Cody, an American soldier, bison hunter, and early frontier showman. Buffalo Bill wrote in his autobiography about the strange beliefs of the Pawnee Indians. While camping with Cody and an Army surgeon, the Indians presented them with very large bones. One of them was supposedly a thighbone from a giant. Cody and the surgeon were amused as they listened to the Pawnee explain the origins of the bone.

Cody writes, "The Indians said the bones were of a race of people who long ago lived in that country. They said these people were three times the size of a man of present day, and were so swift they could run by the side of a buffalo, and taking the animal in one arm, could tear off a leg and eat it as they ran."[8]

He continues:

These giants denied the existence of a Great Spirit, when they heard the thunder or saw the lightning, they laughed and declared that they were greater than either. This so displeased the Great Spirit that he caused a deluge. The water rose higher and higher so that it drove these proud, and conceited giants from the low ground to the hills, and thence to the mountains, but at last even the mountaintops were submerged and then those mammoth men were all drowned. After the flood had subsided, the Great Spirit came to the conclusion that he had made man too large and powerful, and that he would therefore, correct the mistake by creating a race of men of smaller size and less strength. This is the reason, say the Indians, that modern men are small and not like the giants of old. The story has been handed down among the Pawnee for generations, and they claim that this story is a matter of Indian history, but what is its origin no man can say.[9]

The giant bones belonging to Buffalo Bill were eventually given to a museum, which promptly lost them.

According to an article published in the May 13, 1928, edition of the *Humboldt Star,* a nine-foot-tall red-haired mummy was discovered deep inside the Lovelock Cave, located twenty miles south of the town of Lovelock, Nevada. Isolated on top of a high hill, the cave is estimated to be 40 feet deep and 180 feet wide. The Piute Indians told the early Nevadan settlers fantastic stories about the origins of the cave, including tales about their fierce battles with red-haired white giants. In their oral history they claimed to have cornered the remaining giants in Lovelock Cave. Once the giants were trapped, the Piutes blocked the entrance with sagebrush and set it on fire. They reportedly stoked the fire until all the remaining giants had been smothered by smoke.

Further evidence supporting local legends about giants had emerged in 1911 when a mining company plowing for bat guano in Lovelock Cave began to find amazing artifacts. They discovered layers of burned materials and broken arrows that validated the Piutes' claims. Further down they found the remains of giant red-haired mummies, along with strange stone artifacts and shells carved with mysterious symbols. As usual most of these artifacts were either lost or fell into the hands of private collectors who whisked them away. One museum did manage to preserve some of the items discovered at Lovelock Cave.

The Humbolt County Museum at Winnemucca, Nevada, has in its collection a skull from one of the giants. Stan Nielsen, the famed treasure hunter, pilot, and photojournalist, went to investigate this skull with some dental plaster and a camera. The museum curator graciously allowed Nielsen to compare the plaster model of a normal-size man's jaw with a jaw of one of the giants found in the museum's collection. The photographic evidence clearly shows the vast difference in size between the plaster model and the immense jaw from the giant skull. What's more amazing is that anyone can see this skull for themselves by contacting the friendly staff at the Humbolt County Museum. Recent e-mail transactions have verified that some of the sensational Lovelock Cave artifacts, including a giant skull, are being kept in the back room of the museum.

But stories about similar sensational discoveries continue to this very day. An article published online June 29, 2010, by *National Geographic* titled "Diver 'Vanishes' in Portal to Maya Underworld" discusses the recent exploits by the Belize Institute of Archaeology, which was busy exploring the underwater cave system in Belize. Seemingly buried in the article is the important statement made by lead archaeologist Lisa Lucero concerning the discovery of several fossil beds 60 to 90 feet below the surface. While diving and digging through these deep fossil beds, Lucero discovered "femur bones the size of a bowling ball." These giant bones were discovered near elephant tusks and pelvic bones. Lucero admits to leaving the giant bones behind, saying, "We left those in place. We only removed a few small fossils so we can determine, are they fossilized? Or bone? They are definitely fossilized, so we know they have to be of a certain age. But were they here, were these megafauna present during occupation by humans 20,000, 15,000 years ago? Or are they much older?"[10]

The remains of ancient giants in America are scarce, but evidence, both empirical and anecdotal, does exist. By reading the various newspapers and town journals of the 1800s a serious investigator will find a surprising number of stories about discoveries concerning giants. Many tales emerge from mounds that were being excavated by hordes of new frontiersmen moving west along the trail blazed by the Corps of Discovery.

Lewis and Clark's mission was to find a sensible route to the Pacific Ocean, to categorize the plants and animals, to map the land, and to give new names to the rivers and mountains. Most of all, they came to prepare the way for the onslaught of a new civilization built on concepts of progress, change, and exploitation of resources that were utterly alien to the native people. As trusted friends and military men of experience, they were hand-picked by President Jefferson for this monumental mission. Their instructions were precise.

Their meticulous handling, documenting, and recording of data was necessary and vital to their mission. It is therefore inexplicable that the main participant of this journey would have missing dates and gaps in his journal from October 24 to November 17, 1805, and that it would be unclear on what day exactly the expedition reached the Pacific Ocean. The odd and scattered accounts during those days, and up to November 17, suggest that they may have spent some time doing something other than seeking a way to the beach.

Eight

The Hero Returns

The winter spent in Fort Clatsop was a difficult one for the Corps of Discovery. The days were dreary, cloudy, and cold, with little sunlight. The food supply was low, and the explorers had to resort to rationing as the salmon ran out and the bad weather made it impossible to conduct any successful hunting outings. The return trip home weighed heavily on the men's hearts as they contemplated the long journey back and the possible disasters awaiting them.

With low morale attributed to starvation, the Corps of Discovery left Fort Clatsop on March 23, 1806, to face fighting the river currents and falls of the Columbia. Bruised and battered, they decided to ditch their canoes and head inland. They retrieved their horses from the Nez Percé and waited for the mountain snow to melt before riding back to the Continental Divide. Here the corps split into two teams. Lewis wanted to explore the Marias River, which he named after his beloved cousin, and took three men along on this detour. He wanted to research the northern reaches of the Marias, and although he didn't know it at the time, Lewis and his team were wandering into sacred hunting grounds.

The decision to explore this new territory suggests that Lewis was in full military strategist mode and had become focused on achieving the primary goal of discovering a river route to the Pacific. Locating a route between the Marias and Saskatchewan Rivers would have been helpful in cutting into the pockets of Canadian fur traders. The Canadians dominated the lucrative fur trade business, and America was desperate to get a piece of the action. Lewis was looking for a breakthrough to fulfill this part of the expedition's assignment. If he had suffered a mental breakdown at Fort Clatsop, it seems questionable that he would have been so motivated.

Unfortunately the route did not appear, and Lewis had no choice but to continue downriver, where he encountered the Blackfeet tribe. The Blackfeet, who controlled most of the north Saskatchewan River to Canada, noticed the lost white strangers. The natives were heavily armed and known for unprovoked attacks on their neighbors, the Nez Percé and Shoshone.

When the horse-riding warriors approached Lewis, he feared the worst. Outnumbered but alert, Lewis was prepared to fight to the death if the warriors made any attempt to rob him of his papers, survey instruments, or gun. The Blackfeet were shocked to see these white men trotting upon their land and were equally uneasy. The two parties awkwardly shook hands. Lewis knew he was in a vulnerable position, but when the Blackfeet invited him and his men to camp, he had little choice but to agree.

This was the first time they had encountered this tribe, and there were many things Lewis was not aware of. For example, he was unaware that the Blackfeet had been given guns by Canadian and British traders. The Blackfeet's dominance over the Nez Percé and Shoshone depended on this advantage. Lewis made the mistake of telling the Blackfeet about their earlier dealings with the Nez Percé and Shoshone tribes and naively explained how he was arming and cooperating with the Blackfeet's rivals, unknowingly creating a direct threat to their interests. Hoping for peace and a decent night's rest, Lewis offered the Blackfeet some horses and tobacco.

He assigned one man to lookout duty, and Lewis and the others were able to fall asleep. Exhausted, the man on duty also fell asleep. Taking advantage of the situation, a Blackfeet warrior slyly pilfered some of their guns and was making his escape when one of Lewis's men woke in time to see him running. The commotion that ensued ended the fretful rest, and Lewis awoke from a "profound" sleep to a chaotic nightmare. After a chase the young Blackfeet thief was caught by one of Lewis's men. Instead of returning the weapons, the young warrior decided to make a fight out of it. As they wrestled Lewis's man pulled out his knife and plunged it deep into the Blackfeet's chest and killed him.

Moments later the other Blackfeet thieves were rounded up and the guns retrieved. But this was just another distraction as Lewis saw that other Blackfeet were now attempting to steal their horses. Losing their horses would have been an irreparable disaster as this would have left the small band of men alone with no means of escape. Giving his men instruction to shoot if the renegades got brave, Lewis went after the Blackfeet who had taken his horse. Lewis gave chase until he ran out of breath. What followed was the most frightening encounter of his journey. He writes in his journal:

> at the distance of three hundred paces they entered one of those steep nitches in the bluff with the horses before them being nearly out of breath. I could pursue no further, I called to them as I had done several times before that I would shoot them if they did not give me my horse and raised my gun. One of them jumped behind a rock and spoke to the other who turned around and stopped at the distance of 30 steps from me and I shot him through the belly. He fell to his knees and on his right elbow from which position he partly raised himself up and fired at me. And turning himself about crawled in behind a rock, which was a few feet from him. He overshot me. Being bareheaded I felt the wind of his bullet very distinctly.[1]

After the shooting, the rest of the Indians fled. Lewis knew he and his men were now in a world of trouble. An ill-fated diplomatic excursion had ended in death for two Blackfeet and near-disaster for him and his men. The echo of the nearly fatal whizzing bullet left him shaken. He rounded up the men and available horses, and fearful of a revenge party, they rode fast and hard out of there. Lewis left behind a reminder of his presence by placing the Jefferson peace medal around the neck of the dead warrior. He and his men rode frantically back to the Missouri, hoping for a reunion with the rest of the Corps of Discovery.

Meanwhile Clark and his group had entered Crow territory along the Yellowstone River in present-day northern Wyoming. By then it was summer, and the refreshing breeze must have been a welcome change from the chilling Oregon winter, and a sign they were closer to the culmination of the journey.

While Clark and his men were setting up camp on the riverbanks, the Crow amicably approached them. However, their friendliness was a facade. The Crow natives were the most notorious horse thieves of the plains. By morning half of Clark's horses were gone, and not a single Crow could be found. The loss of horses made the journey difficult, because the group had to walk long stretches in the heat until new horses were located.

In contrast to Lewis's troubled exploration of the Missouri and Marias, Clark's trip along the Yellowstone held pleasant surprises and visual wonders. Though he missed discovering Yellowstone Park by about forty miles, Clark did discover monuments recognized by other ancient travelers.

The most memorable one is a giant sandstone pillar containing ancient petroglyphs, which Clark named "Pompy's Tower" after Sacagawea's infant son, whom he had nicknamed "Pompy," which means "little chief." Captain Clark carved the date and his name on the rock, and he detailed in his journal the various images he tried to make out of the petroglyphs. Many of the oldest glyphs have eroded with time, but Clark's signature has been framed and protected by a thin screen. These weren't the only petroglyphs Clark encountered on the return journey. In Kansas, a short distance from the mouth of the Nemaha River, he examined petroglyphs that resembled stars in the night sky.

After camping near the pillar, Clark and his team continued their journey. Surrounded by bison, they had no shortage of food or panoramic views. The ever-stretching skies blanketed them as they rode their bullboats down the Yellowstone River. They stopped periodically so a few of Clark's men could venture into the wilderness to hunt for food. Clark's men weren't the only ones seeking nourishment in the area. Meriwether Lewis and his men had escaped a sure death from the Blackfeet as they hurried down the Missouri. Eager to be reunited with the expedition at the convergence of the Yellowstone and Missouri Rivers, Lewis rode at a blistering pace.

Exhausted and hungry after a long stretch, Lewis took a break from riding and ventured into the woods to hunt. Spotting some elk, Lewis began to aim his rifle when he was shot in the hip by a bullet. He clutched his hip and screamed out in pain. Lewis immediately assumed one of his own men had shot him, but when he didn't hear a response, he feared it might have been hostile natives. Rushing back to the river, he organized the men and moved on. There were no native tribes to be seen in the vicinity, and none of the men ever admitted to shooting him. For Lewis it was just another bad omen, a stack of which seemed to be growing since he had left the Pacific coast. Various theories emerged to explain the shooting. A volume of published speculation suggests that Lewis was mistaken for an elk by a poor-sighted riverman and translator Pierre Cruzatte and shot by mistake.

On August 12, 1806, Lewis reunited with Clark and the rest of the expedition. Relieved and spent, Lewis showed Clark his injury. Fortunately the wound wasn't life threatening. But the bullet had gone straight through, and the mangled flesh had become infected. With the help of natural medicine and rest, Lewis recovered but was in no mood for writing. His frustration is evident as he makes his last journal entry complaining about the pain he suffered from the gunshot wound. Knowing that the distance home was now shorter, he was eager to get into the canoes and sail with the currents back to St. Louis. It is at this point that Lewis assigns all future writing to Clark, and with obvious relief he gives up his role as captain of the expedition. He abandons his sworn duties without much concern and settles back as a spectator.

As Lewis and Clark made their way home during late September the expedition made more important zoological and botanical discoveries. In all, they discovered more than 179 new species of plants and trees and 122 species of animals, birds, and fish.

As the Corps of Discovery glided down the Missouri, the stress from the journey gradually lifted. The explorers had participated in one of the most adventurous and amazing camping trips of all time and had lived to tell the world about it.

It must be restated here that Lewis and Clark were only rediscovering the ancient lands of America. Dr. Barry Fell was one of the figures who championed this notion, and another who paid a price for it.

A Harvard-educated professor, Dr. Fell wrote groundbreaking works on New World epigraphy. This linguistic study consumed Fell as he researched and covered grounds his peers would not. Not surprisingly, the academic establishment ignored his revelations, trying their best to erase him from history with silence or critique.

But when looking into Fell's work it becomes clear he possessed an encyclopedic amount of knowledge, especially on the topics of ancient languages. Fell was far ahead of self-proclaimed experts who restrict their work to a single script or language. Fell studied all languages, and he wrote his first study on the ancient petroglyphs of Polynesia in 1940. His life's work culminated in the publication of a trilogy of controversial books in the 1970s. The most famous of these three books was *America BC*.

In it, based on his studies of ancient rock art, he proposed that Celts, Arabs, Phoenicians, and others had visited and traded with Native Americans long before Columbus. This simple truth was bashed by the academic world, and the facts were kept from the general public. The academics even brought out the big guns from the Smithsonian's anthropology department to write the accepted scholarly rebuttal to Fell's work. Letting the Smithsonian investigate theories of pre-Columbian visitors to America's shores is like letting Charlie Manson investigate the Sharon Tate murders.

It is important to bear in mind that the majority of the early European colonists were uneducated in cultural anthropology, and when they looked at any rock art, they had no idea as to the art's antiquity, its significance, or about the people who had created it. The colonists could barely communicate with the Native Americans about simple survival. This lack of communication resulted in hundreds of years of knowledge waiting undiscovered or unexplored. Fell's work changed all this, or was at least supposed to, before he was condemned.

Some of Fell's work addressed the megalithic stone oddities found throughout the New England states. Known as America's Stonehenge, the ruins found at Mystery Hill, New Hampshire, bear a striking resemblance to those found in England. Some of these stones contained inscriptions that Fell determined to be in the style of ancient Celtic ogham writing. When the inscriptions were translated, Fell discovered they were dedicated to the Celtic sun god, Bel. Bel was also known as Baal and was worshipped by the Phoenicians who came from ancient Palestine. These "eye of Bel" types of engravings have been found inside solar chambers all across New England.

Fell made another bizarre discovery several miles off the coast of Maine, finding a stone inscribed in what he determined to be Goidelic Celtic writing. After deciphering it Fell determined that the tablet spoke of ships sailing from Phoenicia. This provided evidence of what many now assume to be true—that the Phoenicians and Celts were brave seafaring warriors who touched the lands of America before Columbus.

Fell provided another example of intercultural trade in ancient America when he studied a three-hundred-pound chunk of pink granite first discovered in Bourne, Massachusetts, around 1860. Fell was able to identify the letters inscribed on the stone as a variation of the Punic and Iberian alphabets found in ancient Spain. He translated the writing as recording the annexation of modern-day Massachusetts by Hanno the navigator, a commander of Carthage. The Carthaginians were the natural successors to the Phoenicians and continued the tradition of maritime dominance. Hanno was a real historical figure who explored and colonized along the African coast around 500 BCE. He founded several cities and set up trading posts. The Greeks had been referring to his heroic voyages since the tenth century CE. According to the Greeks, Hanno was said to have circumnavigated the Atlantic.

After a lengthy examination of the ruins inhabiting the remote areas of Vermont, Fell was convinced of the importance of his discoveries, writing, "Within ten days we were finding dozens of Ogam inscriptions on another more remote site in central Vermont. It became clear that ancient Celts had built these stone chambers as religious shrines, and the Carthaginian mariners were visitors who were permitted to worship at them and make dedications in their own language to their own gods."[2]

Perhaps Fell's most important contribution to pre-Columbian contact in America was his decipherment of the Davenport Stele. Found in 1874 in a burial mound in Iowa, this stele has been called the Rosetta Stone of the West. Inscribed on this stele were three different types of writing that Fell was able to read. They included Egyptian hieroglyphics, Iberian Punic, and Libyan script. Fell estimated the age of the stele to be ninth century BCE. Another curious stele thought to be of the same age was discovered around 1888 on Long Island, New York, and contains more Egyptian and Libyan script.

This bilingual inscribed tablet referred to an expedition sent from Egypt. Fell suggested that early visitors from Egypt might have traded with the Algonquin Indians and perhaps taught them how to use Egyptian hieroglyphic signs in writing. Fell analyzed the inscriptions and began to compare them with writings of the Algonquin/Micmac Indians of Maine. Using an Indian-language dictionary prepared by a missionary around 1690, Fell noted the clear similarities between the written script of the Algonquin/Micmac Indians and that of ancient Egypt. He concluded that the Micmac language was actually a derivative of ancient Egyptian.

This discovery from a professor at Harvard University should have shaken scholars. Instead the findings have been neglected and assigned to shelves of museums and libraries or buried in basement archives. There have been other Egyptian artifacts discovered in America that shared the same fate. A particularly interesting one is a 9-inch-high Egyptian soapstone statue found in an ancient burial mound in Libertyville, Illinois. Information about this important discovery is only to be found in an obscure *Ancient American* magazine article from 1999. The well-crafted object clearly portrays an Egyptian man holding a shepherd's crook and a flail, both of which are recognizable icons of ancient Egypt.

In 1952 several coins bearing ancient Hebrew iconography were found in Kentucky. Dr. Ralph Marcus of the University of Chicago identified the iconography on the coins as being related to the revolt of the Jews against Rome in 132–135 CE.

In Tennessee several artifacts have turned up bearing Hebrew script, the most important being the Bat Creek Stone, professionally excavated by the Smithsonian mound survey project in Tennessee in 1889. The Bat Creek Stone was unearthed from an undisturbed burial mound by Cyrus Thomas, who initially declared that the curious inscriptions didn't resemble the Cherokee alphabet at all. The stone measures just five inches long and is inscribed with eight Paleo-Hebrew characters dating from about the first or second century CE. Roman coins dating from this period have also been discovered along the Ohio River in Kentucky. However, since the discoverer of these coins in 2009 was a humble fisherman, his claims were denied despite no official study to prove otherwise.

There seems to be no shortage of Roman coins in Kentucky. Once again the establishment chooses its best weapon—silence.

Take, for example, the case in 1963, when a construction engineer found a stockpile of coins while excavating the north bank of the Ohio River. The coins were huddled together in the remains of a disintegrated leather pouch. The discoverer secretly kept most of the coins, but he did give two away to his friend, also an engineer on the project. Thirty years later the engineer's widow brought these two coins to the Falls of the Ohio Museum in Clarksville, Indiana. The museum curator, Troy McCormick, identified one of the coins as a bronze of Claudius II, from 268 CE. The other coin was examined by Mark Lehman, an expert in ancient coins and president of Ancient Coins for Education, Inc. He recognized it as a follis of Maximinus II, from around 300 CE. The Falls of the Ohio Museum had these coins on display for a number of years until it was informed by the state of Indiana that the exhibit conflicted with the state's archaeological policy, claiming there is no documented evidence of pre-Columbian American contacts.

That we know of, Lewis and Clark didn't find any Roman coins on their journey, but they definitely walked the path traveled by a rainbow of ancient peoples.

The Corps of Discovery returned to St. Louis on September 23, 1806, to a roaring celebration. The whole town welcomed Lewis and Clark with a monumental heroes' reception. Lewis was back in good spirits and finally resumed writing, penning a long letter to Thomas Jefferson. In it he detailed an overview of their discoveries, adventures, and safe return home. When Jefferson received the letter a month later, he responded with joy and relief. After the expedition's safe homecoming the corps disbanded.

Dubbed national heroes, the men of the expedition were paid well, and each was given 320 acres of land for his efforts. Some of the men got married and farmed, while others returned to the frontier to trade fur and dig gold. Sacagawea went east at Clark's invitation and formally let her son be raised by Clark. She returned to her village and gave birth to a little girl. Shortly after, she died from an unknown illness. William Clark was given a high position in the government, with which he quickly grew bored. The only member of the expedition who was not rewarded fairly was William Clark's slave, York. Despite his help and commitment to the expedition, William Clark denied York his freedom.

Today we can appreciate the far-reaching magnitude of Lewis and Clark's journey to the West. But at the time, Jefferson's goal to find a river route that linked with the Pacific had failed. His assumption that it would take Americans a hundred generations to settle the West was also wrong. Lewis and Clark opened the floodgates, and after the discovery of gold, the hordes were unleashed. The prairies turned in to farms, the buffalo were hunted to extinction, the Native Americans were killed, and the survivors were rounded up and placed on reservations. The white man's diseases would eventually decimate the populations of the Mandan, Arikaras, and Hidatsa, the hospitable tribes whose friendliness and helpfulness were so crucial to Lewis and Clark and the Corps of Discovery.

The explorers managed an extraordinary feat by surviving the six-thousand-mile excursion. The ramifications of this journey would prove to be monumental. The West they traveled would never be the same.

After resting and recuperating in St. Louis for several months, Lewis departed for Washington in the winter of 1807. Little did he know that the political atmosphere brewing in the heart of Washington would prove to be deadlier than any of the experiences he faced during the expedition.

Nine

Friends in High Places

Upon his arrival Lewis was greeted again with a hero's welcome in Washington, D.C., and Philadelphia. He became the toast of the town and enjoyed his celebrity status. Returning to the familiarity of the White House, Lewis was also welcomed into the home of President Jefferson, where conversations about the expedition and Lewis's personal thoughts and opinions on the discoveries were shared in great detail.

Jefferson, who had always nurtured a spirit of exploration, listened to Lewis's informative accounts as if the president himself had participated in the historical venture. Lewis obtained extra money and land grants for his men, and he was appointed governor of the extensive Louisiana Territory. His experience as a military officer and the popularity he received after the expedition made him a natural for the position. As Lewis prepared his journals for publication he undoubtedly looked forward to his upcoming duties as governor, a job that would further develop his experience for what at the time seemed to point to his eventual calling: the presidency. Regardless of how excited Lewis might have been about his future possibilities, however, he would soon be discouraged by the political infighting brewing. He was thrown into a hornet's nest that made the lands of the Louisiana Territory the original Wild West.

It's important to recognize just how dangerous a time Lewis was living in. The American Revolution had taken place thirty years earlier, and the newly formed United States was still in a relatively vulnerable position, subjected to the direction and edicts of its founders.

In this specific regard the disagreements between Alexander Hamilton and Thomas Jefferson were at a fever pitch. They were famous, potent rivals. Jefferson was aware of Hamilton's allegiance to a nefarious cult that the president believed was plotting a takeover of the young United States by creating a central bank that would control the country's currency. Jefferson was suspicious of Hamilton's association with the Rothschilds and feared betrayal.

It is no secret that most of the founders were in the frequent company of Freemasons. Although he never claimed to be one, Jefferson visited Masonic temples and had high-ranking Masonic friends such as Benjamin Franklin. Jefferson used this access to acquire the knowledge he felt was going to be used against the founders by usurpers who were gearing up for a war.

Both Lewis and Clark were Masons as well. In fact Lewis was known for achieving high rank among American Masons in almost record time. Lewis was elected to the Door of Virtue Lodge in January 1797 and had climbed the ranks to Past Master Mason within three months. By 1799 he had attained status of Royal Arch Mason in Widow's Son Lodge at Milton, Virginia. Shortly thereafter Lewis had been chosen by Jefferson to be his private secretary.

In September of 1808, after being named governor of Louisiana Territory, Lewis helped establish the first Masonic lodge in St. Louis and was named Master of St. Louis Lodge, Number 111. During his time as governor Lewis was active in the lodge and shared duties with his most bitter rival, Frederick Bates, who was a close associate of famed traitor General James Wilkinson. When Lewis left St. Louis on his fateful, final journey, he handed over his Master's role to Bates, who later signed William Clark's Masonic diploma, presumably after Clark was encouraged to join the Masons by Lewis.

Today the so-called Illuminati have become darlings of pop culture. But it wasn't long ago that the mere mention of the words *Illuminati* or *New World Order* was enough to squash a prominent career or, even worse, get a person killed. The danger was even worse in the days of Meriwether Lewis, when the Illuminati's infiltration into the very heart of the country was establishing very strong roots.

George Washington, the first president of the United States, was personally indebted to the Rothschilds, who were instrumental in helping him obtain his position as a land surveyor. George Washington did not oppose the foreign influence of the Illuminati, but he wrote cautionary letters about them. One of these letters, dated October 24, 1798, says:

> It was not my intention to doubt that the doctrines of the Illuminati and the principles of Jacobinism had not spread in the United States. On the contrary, no one is more satisfied of this fact than I am. The idea I meant to convey, was, that I did not believe that the lodges of Freemasons in this country had, as societies, endeavored to propagate the diabolical tenets of the first, or pernicious principles of the latter. That individuals of them may have done it, or that the founder or instruments employed to have found the democratic societies in the United States may have had this object, and actually had a separation of the people from their government in view, is too evident to be questioned.[1]

This secret battle continued at the universities as well. On July 4, 1812, Joseph Willard, then president of Harvard University, delivered a speech in Lancaster, New Hampshire, explaining:

> There is sufficient evidence that a number of societies, of the Illuminati, have been established in this land of Gospel light and civil liberty, which were first organized from the grand society, in France. They are doubtless secretly striving to undermine all our ancient institutions, civil and sacred. These societies are closely leagued with those of the same Order, in Europe; they have all the

same object in view. The enemies of all order are seeking our ruin. Should infidelity generally prevail, our independence would fall of course. Our republican government would be annihilated.[2]

Alexander Hamilton served as secretary of the Treasury under George Washington during 1789–1795 and learned a great deal about the banking system. This knowledge helped him form the Federalist Party, primarily made up of bankers who advocated a strong central government. Naturally the Anti-Federalists favored states' rights and remained true to the original ideas fought for by the founders. Because Hamilton was a founder himself his perceived betrayal was an even greater offense. Jefferson was conscious of this and had anticipated an eventual showdown with Hamilton.

Before Jefferson was able to develop a strategy to handle Hamilton, the wheels of destruction began turning. The infamous House of Rothschild had its sights set on America. It is difficult to unravel historical facts about the Rothschilds from the volumes of paranoid, anti-Semitic agitprop that seems to have been recycled continuously since the 1800s.

Put simply, the Rothschild banking family has been the source of an extraordinary amount of absurd propaganda. For centuries proponents have promoted the idea that Jewish banking houses in Europe, and therefore the Jewish race, were responsible for manipulation of financial markets that led to widespread and terrible poverty. This theory has been used by politicians for centuries to woo populist voters and by modern authors to sell a lot of books to people who don't know any better.

Established by a goldsmith named Amschel Bauer in Frankfurt, Germany, in 1743 this group of elite bankers had already managed to monopolize much of the wealth of Germany and England. They succeeded by creating what we know of today as "fractional reserve banking." The House of Rothschild learned fast that loaning money to people was small change. The real cash was to be made by loaning money to governments, ensuring the money would always be covered by public taxes. Amschel was a pioneer in the art of dominating nations by gaining access to their banking institutions. You needn't look any further than Amschel himself, who famously declared in 1790, "Let me issue and control a nation's money and I care not who writes the laws."[3]

In the 1700s Britain was a powerful nation sinking in massive amounts of debt. This was in part attributed to the Rothschilds takeover of local finance institutions and forming the Bank of England. The House of Rothschild also developed plans to extract money from the American colonies. The colonies were flourishing during this time. They controlled their own destiny by using colonial script as purchasing power. The colonies were not in debt to anybody or any entity and were free from the Bank of England. This oversight was not tolerated by the powers of the time, especially the English bankers. Through their privately owned Bank of England they wrote the Currency Act of 1764 and forced Parliament to pass it.

Although never cited in any traditional history books, the Currency Act truly sparked the Revolutionary War. The act made it illegal for the American colonies to print their own money. Even worse, it forced them to pay taxes to Britain in silver and gold. This brutal blow by the bankers ended the growing economic success the colonies were experiencing through independent trade and forced the eventual showdown over what became known as Taxation Without Representation.

For the first time the founders were forced to consider raising arms against the crown. In his autobiography Ben Franklin recalls the gloom in the air.

> In one year, the conditions were so reversed that the era of prosperity ended, and a depression set in, to such an extent that the streets of the Colonies were filled with unemployed. The colonies would gladly have borne the little tax on tea and other matters had it not been that England took away from the colonies their money, which created unemployment and dissatisfaction. The inability of the colonists to

get power to issue their own money permanently out of the hands of George III and the international bankers was the prime reason for the Revolutionary War.[4]

Britain wasn't worried about fighting a war with America. The British government reasoned it would be an easy victory; however, what it wasn't counting on was America's use of guerrilla warfare tactics learned from the Native Americans. With a little help from the French navy the colonists shook up the world by defeating the British army—but not before George Washington was tricked into taking a loan from someone he trusted. While the war was on the verge of being lost, Washington borrowed from fellow founder Alexander Hamilton.

Hamilton was acting as a Rothschild agent, and this one shrewd move essentially won the war for the bankers. When the war was over the colonies were granted independence, but with Hamilton's sly maneuvering the House of Rothschild already had its proverbial foot in the door. After the Revolutionary War there was a huge debt to be paid, and Hamilton wasted no time in setting up the First Bank of the United States in 1791, shortly after Benjamin Franklin's death. This bank was privately owned and secretly belonged to the Rothschild consortium. Benjamin Franklin understood the dangers of a privately owned central bank controlling the issue of the nation's currency.

Jefferson disagreed with Hamilton strongly about a national bank, believing it would acquire too much power over the government. He said at the time that he considered a private bank issuing public currency and the creation of perpetual national debt to be more of a threat to America than any army.

Hamilton thought the opposite, convinced banks would play a vital role in American's future. He championed his position by declaring it was better to have American banks doing the lending than British banks. Of course he never mentioned that the same people who owned the banks of England had made the move to own the first American bank as well.

In addition to their quarrels over banking, Hamilton and Jefferson disagreed on the projected path of the American future. Jefferson believed that liberty and freedom were the greatest virtues a society could have and that the nation could be sustained by an agrarian society made up of independent farmers. Hamilton laughed at what he referred to as Jefferson's "outdated" vision and was convinced that an agricultural economy would keep America poor. Hamilton and the powers he worked for were not interested in being peaceful farmers. They were intent on building nations into world powers, sustained by trade and manufacturing.

Jefferson faced a tremendous challenge in keeping America safe from Hamilton. Hamilton wanted to install an American king and even created the concept of "implied powers," which was a clause used to cover any governmental action not enumerated in the Constitution. Through his own Federalist Party, Hamilton had infiltrated all branches of the government and gained a near monopoly of the judicial system. Dedicated to achieving a simple goal, Hamilton wanted to increase the federal government's power over the states. This was never a popular idea, as the voters said "No" time and time again. Even though Hamilton suffered electoral defeat after defeat, he wasn't discouraged and knew the original plans were being carried out clandestinely. As Jefferson paced the grounds of the White House, he knew he was surrounded on all sides by dark forces.

However successful Hamilton was in gaining access to and control over America's newly formed government, it wouldn't last long enough for him to enjoy it. Aaron Burr killed Hamilton in what may be the most famous duel in American history. With the death of Hamilton, Jefferson had one less enemy to worry about. But Hamilton's death caused mass commotion and hysteria as Burr, Jefferson's disgraced vice president, went on the lam.

Less well known as an agent for the British central banking advocates was Nicholas Biddle. Biddle was a brilliant lawyer, publisher, financier, and at the vanguard of American efforts to establish a central banking system. Biddle was every bit as responsible as Hamilton for founding the First Bank of the United States. When the First Bank's charter expired, it was revived and led by Biddle until Andrew Jackson vetoed its charter, leading to its implosion in 1843. Jackson believed that the future of America was in jeopardy thanks to the influence of foreign banking interests such as the Rothschilds.

While all of this was going on, news began to circulate in the colonial streets that the seemingly crazed General James Wilkinson was gearing up for an invasion of Mexico. The triumphs of Lewis and Clark quickly faded from public consciousness as news of Wilkinson's plans spread.

Growing up poor, Wilkinson had joined the American Revolutionary Army. Owing to his reckless bravado and cunning, he became a general by the age of twenty. He never seemed to care about the ideals he was supposed to be fighting for. He did, however, seem particularly interested in being paid. That attitude didn't sit well with the other founders, but the general was tolerated because he was considered a great commander and a charismatic leader. None of the founders trusted him, but they kept him around out of loyalty. Wilkinson would eventually lead the Army longer than any general of his era, but his oversized ego and lofty ambitions outgrew his duties to America.

Wilkinson had become a land speculator and, through his newly acquired connections, acted as a spy and conspired with Spanish agents concerning the lands along the Mississippi. His treachery wasn't fully realized until the Spanish-American War, when U.S. troops captured the Spanish archives in Cuba. In the archives they found astonishing information regarding Wilkinson's role as an agent working for Spain.

After the Spanish left the picture Wilkinson devised a new plot with then Vice President Aaron Burr to organize an unofficial invasion of Texas. His plans failed to manifest again and again as the playing field changed overnight due to events in Europe and the Louisiana Purchase.

Spain could no longer pay attention to the colonies thanks to Napoleon's fiery invasion. But when one door closes, another opens. At least it was so for Wilkinson, who, after the Louisiana Purchase, was appointed governor of the new territory by President Thomas Jefferson. While serving as governor Wilkinson sent secret reconnaissance missions deep into Texas territory. Wilkinson was looking for gold and new routes into Mexico. He was going to invade and overthrow the Spanish with or without support from Congress, and he needed all the resources he could acquire. One way of getting the bullets he needed was to secure the large lead mines found south of St. Louis.

Congress felt that the immense fortunes to be made in lead mining operations south of St. Louis could pay for the Louisiana Purchase within five years. But the land speculators who had been conniving with the Spanish for control of these mines weren't about to give them up so easily. It conveniently happened that the man appointed to govern these mines for the United States was the treacherous General Wilkinson.

Wilkinson's right-hand man was another chief troublemaker for President Jefferson. Probably the most feared man in the territory, John Smith T. was an aggressive land swindler looking to acquire all the lead mines he came across. He was reputed to have killed fifteen men in duels and always carried four pistols, a Bowie knife, and a rifle. He could provide the remaining lead needed for Wilkinson's invasion of Mexico, but before they could make the move Jefferson removed Wilkinson from his gubernatorial duties.

Wilkinson was furious over his demotion when, after the capture of Aaron Burr, fingers began pointing in Wilkinson's direction as a coconspirator. Wilkinson's removal, and the government's subsequent clampdown on the mines, left the Louisiana territories in a chaotic state. Crime and corruption were everywhere, and the whole area needed to be cleaned out.

This was the obstacle facing Lewis as he prepared to succeed Wilkinson as the new governor of Louisiana. But Lewis was idealistic and optimistic and reportedly looked forward to taking out the trash corrupting the Louisiana territory.

Strangely, Lewis then fell silent for an extended period, much to the dismay of Jefferson and others who awaited the publication of his journals.[5] Various theories have emerged regarding the delay, including that Lewis was given time to recuperate by Jefferson; that he was actively searching for a wife; and that he fell victim to alcoholism, disease, or some other debilitation. Scholars generally concede that a clear answer to what happened to Lewis during this time is unlikely to ever emerge.

This mysterious delay also resulted in scores of volumes of the journals going missing. Gary Moulton, professor and editor of one volume of the published journals of Lewis and Clark, suggests that throughout the years growing evidence indicates that much of what Lewis and Clark wrote about the westward journey was lost.

> Over the years, numerous documents of the expedition have come to light, some in the most unexpected places. . . . These discoveries seem to support the notion of other lost items yet to be found. No hope of discovery ranks so high as the hope of finding Meriwether Lewis's diaries, which would fill the large gaps in his writing during and about the expedition.[6]

What those journal entries contained, and what truths they may have revealed about the fate of their author, remains a mystery.

The other strange anomaly that has come to light are the mysterious gaps in Lewis's journals, which are extensive and have vexed scholars for two centuries. Lewis made no journal entries during the first portion of the journey, for example, from May 14, 1804, until April 7, 1805, when the corps left Fort Mandan. This nearly yearlong gap during what should have been an enthusiastic beginning is especially curious. Some speculate that Lewis was taking field notes or keeping personal journals that he planned to transfer to official notebooks later and that his collection of unofficial inscriptions was then lost.

Letters from Lewis to Jefferson suggest that some kinds of journals were kept during the stay at Fort Mandan. Lewis, for example, mentioned a "correct" copy of a journal that he intended to send back to Washington prior to departing from Fort Mandan. Later he sent another letter to Jefferson promising a proper journal to be delivered by canoe to an outpost on the Missouri River. No journal was ever found. Several other sets of writings did materialize, however: lists of herb specimens, mineral deposits, geologic features, astronomical observations, a weather diary, and other notes. Some of these notes are attributed to other members of the party or are considered collaborative efforts between Lewis and Clark, who may have decided to stray from Jefferson's explicit instructions that they both keep detailed and extensive records.

Others speculate that some of Lewis's journals were lost at various points along the journey. One theory suggests that Lewis's early writings were lost along with Clark's during a sudden storm that rocked the vessel the corps was traveling in shortly after departing Fort Mandan. Clark's notes were known to have been lost, but no mention is made of Lewis or his journals during the incident.

Other long gaps include time on the Ohio and Mississippi Rivers from September 19 to November 11, 1803; a stretch from November 28, 1803, until May 14, 1804; inconsistent entries from August 26, 1805, to January 1, 1806; and a long stretch from August 13, 1806, until the end of the journey. In total there were more than four hundred days of entries missing from Lewis's journals between May 1804, and September 1806. Only the gap beginning on August 13, after Lewis was mysteriously shot in the thigh, has a plausible and evident explanation.

Though it is rarely mentioned in historical accounts of the journey, most scholars involved in collecting, editing, and publishing the journals of the Corps of Discovery conclude that tales of the journey are crafted from a convoluted patchwork of documents: field notes, field journals and notebooks, diary writings, scraps of paper, other various records, and a great deal of conjecture and supposition.

At least eight men were believed to have kept records: Lewis, Clark, privates Joseph Whitehouse and Robert Frazer, sergeants Patrick Glass, John Ordway, Charles Floyd, and Nathaniel Pryor. All but Ordway returned only partial records of the journey. Clark missed nine days in February 1805 while hunting for game. Gass's original journal went missing before a controversial and paraphrased version of it was published in 1807. Though it is assumed he kept some kind of records, no evidence of any documents recorded by Pryor ever appeared. Floyd kept regular entries until his death on August 20, 1804. Private Whitehouse's diary had several gaps and terminates without explanation on November 6, 1805. Ordway kept the most consistent records regarding the events of the day but didn't keep extensive *scientific* records.

Curiously, Lewis's diaries are not included among the works compiled to create the tale of Lewis and Clark's great journey. During a time when the journals were being compiled and prepared for publishing, correspondence between Jefferson, Clark, and one of the first editors of the corps' collective journals, Nicholas Biddle, mention no concern about Lewis's missing diaries.

It is important to note that at this time that Biddle was not yet embroiled in efforts to revive America's central banking system but was likely already in bed with the Rothschilds and the Federalists. Despite a preponderance of missing documents, stories of the corps began circulating in 1806 via newspapers, word of mouth, and government documents, including Jefferson's first report to Congress of the journey. In 1808, with the help of schoolteacher David M'Keehan, the journals of Patrick Gass were published amid public and private protest by Lewis.

Biddle was the first to publish an authorized, official account of the journals kept by Lewis and Clark, albeit a paraphrased narrative and not an edited reprinting of the journals. Biddle was chosen by Clark and several advisors to take on the task that Clark conceded he was not literate enough to complete. At the time Biddle was a young Philadelphia lawyer, editor, and publisher and was considered to be qualified to take on the massive project. At first Biddle refused the job offered to him by Clark but was later convinced by one of Lewis's mentors, botanist Benjamin Smith Barton, to accept the assignment.

With the help of Clark, Biddle began work on the project in 1810, supplementing the collective, remaining journals of the corps with face-to-face interviews with Clark, who provided a wealth of additional material from memory during interviews conducted in Fincastle, Virginia. Biddle then returned to Philadelphia to complete the project.

In June 1811 Biddle finished the manuscript but delayed publishing the work because the chosen publishing house, Conrad, had recently gone bankrupt. Biddle shopped the manuscript around but eventually passed the project off to one of his cohorts at the *Port Folio* magazine, Paul Allen. At the time Biddle said he was overwhelmed by duties in the Pennsylvania state legislature, at *Port Folio,* and in his own law practice.

In 1814 the two-volume *History Of The Expedition Under The Command Of Captains Lewis And Clark, To The Sources Of The Missouri, Thence Across The Rocky Mountains And Down The River Columbia To The Pacific Ocean. Performed During The Years 1804–5–6. By order of the Government Of The United States* was published. Strangely, Biddle's name did not appear on the book, which bore the byline "prepared for the press by Paul Allen, Esquire." Scholars generally consider this edition the first published work to provide a reliable account of the travels of the Corps of Discovery and refer to it as the "Biddle/Allen edition." It is generally accepted that Biddle took some literary liberties with the story, including a number of omissions regarding some of Lewis's checkered history, such as his six court-martials while serving in the military, and a generalized effort to craft the narrative into a rousing frontier tale.

In April of 1818 Biddle claimed to have returned all the journals except Ordway's to agents of the American Philosophical Society. Ordway's journal was considered to have been rich with narrative about the daily exploits of the Corps, including strange details such as their encounters with legendary Welsh natives. Since then a number of journals and papers have appeared that indicate Biddle and others may have kept, lost, or miscataloged a number of the original journals given to them to edit.

In 1903 Reuben Gold Thwaites, editor of the centennial edition of the journals, received previously unknown Clark diaries and papers from Clark's descendants. In 1915 Ordway's journal and several of Lewis and Clark's missing journals were found among some of Biddles old papers. In 1953 Clark's field notes were discovered in a rolltop desk in Minnesota. Thwaites very clearly believed that many of the remaining missing documents, such as Lewis's diaries, were lost shortly after his death in Tennessee.

In an essay that first appeared in *Montana: The Magazine of Western History,* Gary Moulton, editor of a later edition of the Lewis and Clark journals writes,

> These discoveries seem to support the notion of other lost items yet to be found. No hope of discovery ranks so high as the hope of finding Meriwether Lewis's diaries, which would fill the large gaps in his writing during and about the expedition. This essay looks at Lewis's known journals, considers where gaps might be filled with the discovery of new materials, and concludes that there are few possibilities of new finds. To a large degree, these considerations are interpretative and speculative and the conclusions are tentative. We can only hope that more of Lewis's writings are still to be found.[7]

Ten

The Murder of Meriwether Lewis

In June 2009, two centuries after his mysterious death, collateral descendants of Meriwether Lewis launched a website as part of a campaign to exhume and examine the explorer's remains. The announced goal was simple: use modern forensic techniques to determine once and for all whether Lewis died by his own hand, or by someone else's. Lewis's family has worked for more than a decade to secure from the federal National Park Service permission for the exhumation and proper reburial. The campaign encourages concerned Americans to write letters to the secretary of the U.S. Department of the Interior, which oversees the National Park Service, which controls the land in Tennessee where Lewis is buried.

Lewis's family began to bang loudly a drum that has been beating consistently since Lewis's mysterious death at an inn along the historic Natchez Trace roadway. This renewed interest in Lewis's true fate has caused substantial uproar among historians, government officials, academics, and armchair experts as they review a patchwork collection of documents, reports, and various pieces of evidence. All continue to draw a variety of conclusions based on that same evidence. Some say Lewis committed suicide, succumbing to a lifelong battle with depression, bipolar disorder, alcoholism, malaria, syphilis, or some combination thereof.

Others are certain bandits murdered him, and yet others are equally certain that he was murdered as part of an assassination plot carried out by high-ranking officials of the burgeoning U.S. government. If one thing is clear, it is that Lewis's death has come to represent a growing distrust of American history as presented and popularized.

Lewis was just thirty-two years old when he returned from the landmark exploration. The celebrations following the adventurers' return masked the fact that Lewis had returned to an America rife with political turmoil. Upon returning, Lewis and Clark did not waste time in traveling east to debrief President Thomas Jefferson. The explorers were welcomed as heroes wherever they went and spent weeks touring, testifying, and receiving royal treatment. Following a string of celebrations and official inquiries Jefferson rewarded the explorers' accomplishments with instant appointment to high political office.

As we know, Lewis was named governor of the tumultuous Upper Louisiana Territory. Clark was appointed brigadier general of the militia and superintendent of Indian Affairs for the same region, serving alongside Frederick Bates, who was named secretary of the Upper Louisiana Territory to serve under Lewis. Clark and Bates quickly left for St. Louis to begin their work. Lewis, in turn, left to wrap up some business in Philadelphia, where he intended to publish volumes and volumes of journals recorded by the Corps of Discovery during their journey. Lewis searched for a publisher and began looking for artists to illustrate the compiled works. The journals and field notes remained in St. Louis, waiting for Lewis to arrive and prepare them for publication.

Official records of Lewis's life during the next four months are sparse. A letter from Lewis to old friend Mahlon Dickerson suggests that Lewis spent time celebrating and socializing during his stay in Philadelphia and that he may have sparked a romance and proposed marriage to a woman he met there. Lewis later returned to Virginia and made a round of official visits while hosted by President Jefferson at the White House. He also visited with his mother, Lucy Lewis Marks. Details of his time in Virginia end there. Some scholars speculate that he attended the treason trial of Aaron Burr in Richmond, Virginia, at Jefferson's request.

On March 8, 1807—a full year after he was awarded the position— Lewis arrived in St. Louis to begin his appointed duties as governor of Upper Louisiana. His mysterious absence has never been satisfactorily explained. A letter from Jefferson sent during the interim suggests that he was frustrated and concerned about Lewis's absence. The letter, dated July 17, 1807, reads, "Since I parted with you from Albemarle in Sep. last [1806] I have never had a line from you nor I believe has the Secretary of War with which you have much connection through the Indian department." Expressing concern about publication of the expedition journals, he wrote, "We have no tidings yet of the forwardness of your printer. I hope the first part will not be delayed much longer."[1]

Lewis is reported to have taken on his duties as governor with enthusiasm, but he struggled to manage the chaotic political circumstances he had inherited. Secretary Bates is characterized as having it in for Lewis, who he considered a political rival and perhaps usurper of his rightful role as governor of the Louisiana Territory, and is said to have worked hard to undermine Lewis's efforts as governor. Bates may also have harbored some resentment toward Lewis. Years earlier Bates had applied to become Jefferson's private secretary, but Lewis was chosen in his stead.

Meanwhile references to his efforts in letters exchanged between Jefferson and other leaders suggest that Lewis developed a drinking problem. Other letters mark his occasional "melancholia," which many observers suggest was a reference to clinical depression or late stage of syphilis. When James Madison became president in 1809 Jefferson's cabinet was replaced, and Lewis's great ally was no longer able to lend presidential support. Madison's appointed secretary of war, William Eustis, complicated efforts in Louisiana by refusing to pay expense vouchers. Lewis is said to have paid government expenses from his own pocket, spiraling downward into severe financial trouble.

In the fall of 1809, Lewis made a special trip to Washington to settle his disputes with the War Department and to revive efforts to publish his journals. Lewis left St. Louis by boat on September 4, 1809, with plans to travel the Mississippi to New Orleans and then travel by sea to Washington, D.C. Reports from Fort Pickering commander Captain Gilbert Russell suggest that Lewis's health and mental stability were deteriorating. After he arrived at Fort Pickering, near Memphis, Tennessee, Russell relayed that members of the boat crew reported that Lewis had twice attempted to kill himself. Russell was allegedly so alarmed at Lewis's condition that he refused to let him leave until his health improved. During that time Lewis decided to travel to Washington by land. (Lewis said he changed his plans because he was afraid his expedition journals would fall into the hands of the British at sea.) His plan was to leave Fort Pickering for the Natchez Trace, a rough road that stretched 450 miles from Natchez, Mississippi, to Nashville, Tennessee. From there Lewis could take the road to Washington, D.C.

While Lewis continued his compulsory recovery at Fort Pickering, Major James Neelly, agent to the Chickasaw Nation and a close ally of Wilkinson, arrived and agreed to travel with Lewis. By then Lewis's health was reported to have improved enough for him to travel. Lewis left Fort Pickering with Neelly and two servants. One of them, John Pernier, was Lewis's personal servant. The other, an unnamed black man, was Neelly's travel companion.

Shortly after an optimistic departure Neelly reported that Lewis's health had begun to deteriorate. The party rested at the Chickasaw Indian agency and then continued on toward Nashville on the morning of October 10. Neelly stayed behind to look for some horses that had strayed while Lewis and the others went on ahead. That evening, Lewis's party arrived at Grinder's Stand, a roadside inn about seventy miles southeast of Nashville. Lewis and his travel companions checked in with the intention of waiting for Neelly.

Early the next morning, on October 11, Meriwether Lewis died in his room from two gunshot wounds and what appeared to be a series of knife wounds.

Immediate details of the discovery of Lewis's body and the circumstances surrounding his death are largely contained in a single letter from Neelly. His letter to Thomas Jefferson, and subsequent letters sent by friends and associates of Lewis, all seem to have been based on the accounts of Mrs. Grinder, at whose house Lewis stayed. Those accounts, due to the pace of communication, situational complications, and the remoteness of the site of Lewis's demise, were collected and delivered to government officials, including Jefferson, during a period of several years.

The first and most immediate report came from Neelly who, appointed to his position as agent to the Chickasaw Nation by Wilkinson, was suspiciously absent during Lewis's deadly ordeal and was not an eyewitness.

Three months after Lewis's death and Neely's report, Fort Pickering Captain Gilbert Russell, another Wilkinson appointee, wrote two letters to former president Thomas Jefferson, providing further details of Lewis's death. Russell's descriptions of Lewis's health when he arrived at Fort Pickering, along with other descriptions of the explorer's overall health, became the foundation for assertions that Lewis committed suicide.

In the first letter, dated January 4, 1810, Russell described Lewis's condition when he arrived at the fort, noting that he had detained Lewis for his own protection.

The second letter, dated January 31, 1810, contained more details and suggests that Lewis was struggling with a severe drinking problem that seemed to subside during Lewis's compulsory stay at Fort Pickering. Russell then accused Neelly of encouraging Lewis to drink again after they left the fort. "Instead of preventing the Govr from drinking or putting him under restraint advised him to it," Russell wrote, "and from everything I can learn gave the man every chance to seek an opportunity to destroy himself. And from the statement of Grinder's wife where he killed himself I can not help believing that Purney [John Pernier, Lewis's servant] was rather aiding and abetting in the murder than otherwise."[2]

Author and historian Eldon G. Chuinard, who calls Lewis his hero, calls into question the allegation that Lewis was deranged at the time, inferring that Russell had concocted the story. He notes a letter written by Lewis on September 22, 1809—just two weeks before his death—to Amos Stoddard, commandant of Upper Louisiana. The letter, says Chuinard, appears to be written by a very lucid Lewis.

> The entire letter is a lucid, coherent statement written when he was supposed to have mental derangement while coming down the Mississippi and during his first days at Fort Pickering. . . . Also in the letter he says, "You will direct me at the City of Washington until the last of December, after which I expect I shall be on my return to St. Louis." This does not sound like a "mentally depressed" person. A return to his duties in St. Louis was clearly on his mind—not suicide.[3]

Historical investigator Kira Gale goes even further to discredit Russell's reports, speculating that they were forgeries produced by Wilkinson. The assertion that Russell's letters were forged was confirmed by handwriting experts during a coroner's inquest conducted in 1996. Gale suggests that these were the very letters that convinced both William Clark and Thomas Jefferson that their friend had committed suicide.

> After his friend's death, Clark received letters citing suicide attempts by Lewis while he was en route to Fort Pickering and 15 days of mental derangement while he was at the fort. It was enough to convince him at the time. But most likely, these letters were forgeries created by General Wilkinson to mislead Clark. Clark thought the letters were written by Captain Gilbert Russell, the commander of Fort Pickering (today's Memphis, Tennessee), where Lewis spent two weeks in September.
>
> Lewis died under mysterious circumstances on the Natchez Trace

on October 11, 1809 after leaving Fort Pickering. Clark wrote to his brother Jonathan Clark on November 26, 1809 with news of Lewis's suicide attempts and mental derangement—information contained in the letters Clark had received, supposedly written by Captain Russell. These letters from Russell have never been found, so the handwriting cannot be analyzed. However, we have two authentic letters written by Captain Russell to President Thomas Jefferson in January, 1810. These letters to the President provided a wealth of detail, but they contain no report of prior suicide attempts while en route to the fort, no report of 15 days in a state of mental derangement while Lewis was at the fort, and no report of a second will written at the fort. All things Captain Russell would surely have reported to the President if they were true.[4]

Further details of Lewis's demise appeared in a letter from Alexander Wilson to a mutual friend. Wilson was a well-known ornithologist and friend of Lewis and had agreed to complete the bird illustrations for Lewis's published journals. Two years after Lewis's body was discovered, while traveling the Natchez Trace, Wilson interviewed Mrs. Grinder. He recounted the conversation in a letter to Alexander Lawson.

Dated May 28, 1811, it reads:

Next morning (Sunday) I rode six miles to a man's of the name of Grinder, where our poor friend Lewis perished. In the same room where he expired, I took down from Mrs. Grinder the particulars of that melancholy event, which affected me extremely. This house or cabin is seventy-two miles from Nashville, and is the last white man's as you enter the Indian country. Governor Lewis, she said, came there about sun-set, alone, and inquired if he could stay for the night; and, alighting, brought his saddle into the house. He was dressed in a loose gown, white, striped with blue. On being asked if he came alone, he replied that there were two servants behind, who would soon be up. He called for some spirits, and drank a very little. When the servants arrived, one of whom was a negro, he inquired for his powder, saying he was sure he had some powder in a canister. The servant gave no distinct reply, and Lewis, in the mean while walked backwards and forwards before the door, talking to himself. Sometimes, she said, he would seem as if he were walking up to her; and would suddenly wheel round, and walk back as fast as he could. Supper being ready he sat down, but had not eat but a few mouthfuls when he started up speaking to himself in a violent manner. At these times, she says, she observed his face to flush as if it had come on him in a fit. He lighted his pipe, and drawing a chair to the door sat down, saying to Mrs. Grinder in a kind tone of voice, "Madam this is a very pleasant evening." He smoked for some time, but quitted his seat and traversed the yard as before. He again sat down to his pipe, seemed again composed and casting his eyes wishfully towards the west, observed what a sweet evening it was. Mrs. Grinder was preparing a bed for him; but he said he would sleep on the floor, and desired the servant to bring the bear skins and buffaloe robe, which were immediately spread out for him; and it being now dusk the woman went off to the kitchen, and the two men to the barn, which stands about two hundred yards off. The kitchen is only a few paces from the room where Lewis was, and the woman being considerably alarmed by the behavior of her guest could not sleep but listened to him walking backwards and forwards, she thinks for several hours, and talking aloud, as she said, "like a lawyer," She then heard the report of a pistol, and something fall heavily on the floor, and the words "O Lord." Immediately afterwards she heard another pistol, and in a few minutes she hear him at her door calling out "O madam! Give me some water, and heal my wounds." The logs being open, and unplastered, she saw him stagger back and fall against a stump that stands between the kitchen and room. He crawled for some distance, raised himself by the side of a tree, where he sat about a minute. He once more got to the room; afterwards he came to the kitchen door, but did not speak; she then heard him scraping the bucket with a gourd for water, but it appears that this cooling element was denied the dying man! As soon as day broke and not before, the terror of the woman having permitted him to remain for two hours in this most deplorable situation, she sent two of her children to the barn, her husband not being at home, to bring the servants; and on going in they found him lying on the bed; he uncovered his side and shewed them where the bullet had entered; a piece of the forehead was blown off, and had exposed the brains, without having bled much. He begged they would take his rifle and blowout his brains, and he would give them all the money he had in his trunk. He often said, "I am no coward, but I am so strong, so hard to die." He begg'd the servant [John Pernier] not to be afraid of him, for that he would not hurt him. He expired in about two hours, or just as the sun rose above the trees. He lies buried close by the common path, with a few loose rails thrown over his grave. I gave Grinder money to put a post fence round it, to shelter it from the hogs, and from the wolves; and he gave me his written promise he would do it. I left this place in a very melancholy mood, which was not much allayed by the prospect of the gloomy and savage wilderness which I was just entering alone.[5]

Biographer and editor of one of the earliest accounts of Lewis's adventures, Dr. Elliot Coues describes the account given by Wilson of Lewis's death as the one likely to be most accurate. He explains that because of Wilson's scientific training and experience as a researcher, the accuracy of his account should be considered highly, despite the amount of time that lapsed between Lewis's death and the report. What he doubts, however, is the story provided by Mrs. Grinder, which he characterizes as preposterous at best. He also questions strongly the final memoir written by Jefferson. In fact, Coues was so certain that the claim of suicide was bogus, he wrote his own supplement to Jefferson's memoir of Lewis:

. . . Jefferson's Memoire of Lewis is a noble and fitting tribute, leaving little to be desired as a contemporaneous biography. It has been accepted as authoritative and final, and has furnished the basis of every memoir of Lewis I have seen. . . . What else I have to say concerns not Lewis' life, but the circumstances of his death; and certain subsequent events. . . . The affirmation of suicide, though made without qualification, has not passed unchallenged into history. . . . Undoubtedly Jefferson wrote in the light of all evidence that had reached him in 1813; but it appears that his view of the case was far from that of persons who lived in the vicinity of the scene at the time.

There is no more room to doubt Wilson's painstaking correctness than there is reason for doubting his veracity. But the narrative of Mrs. Grinder is very extraordinary. A woman who could do as she said she did, after hearing and seeing what she testifies, must be judged "fit for treason, stratagem, and spoils," and not to be believed under oath. The story is wildly improbable on its face; it does not hang together; there is every sign it is a concoction on the part of an accomplice in crime, either before or after the event. On the theory that Mrs. Grinder was privy to a plot to murder Governor Lewis, and therefore had her own part to play in the tragedy, even if that part were a passive one—or on the theory that, becoming afterward cognizant of the murder, she told a story to shield the actual criminal or criminals—on either of these theories we could understand Mrs. Grinder; otherwise her story is simply incredible. Yet it is upon such evidence as this that the imputation of suicide rests.[6]

As Coues points out, the details of Mrs. Grinder's story are hard to believe. Lewis did indeed seem to have been worried and agitated about something. But why would a woman, who managed a stop along a notoriously dangerous stretch of road, have been unable to sleep over such a thing? Why, upon hearing pistol shots, a thud, and cries for help, would she simply peer through the cracks of her kitchen wall to investigate? When she saw Lewis crawling, falling, struggling, why didn't she aid him? Why wait two hours after shots were fired to raise an alarm? Why send a pair of children to ask servants, who had heard nothing, to investigate? Why did they do nothing as Lewis begged and bribed, for two hours, for them to put him out of his misery? Moreover, as noted by Chuinard, the story told by Grinder does not constitute a reasonable medical probability, no matter how strong Lewis's constitution was.

Despite the implausibility of the reported circumstances, and the knowledge that the first reports came from Neelly and Russell—both allies of Lewis's sworn enemy Wilkinson—it appears that those were the very details upon which Lewis's three closest friends, Thomas Jefferson, William Clark, and Mahlon Dickerson, accepted the notion that he had committed suicide.

In a letter to his brother Jonathan, William Clark wrote, "I fear O! I fear the weight of his mind has overcome him."

Dickerson mourned Lewis's death in his diary and did not question the explanation of suicide.

> While he lived with me in Washington, I observed at times sensible depressions of mind. . . . During his western expedition the constant exertion which that required of all the faculties of body & mind, suspended these distressing affections; but after his establishment in St. Louis in sedentary occupations they returned upon him with redoubled vigor, and began seriously to alarm his friends. He was in a paroxym of one of these when his affairs rendered it necessary for him to go to Washington.[7]

From those few statements and conclusions derive countless books, official reports, biographies, and dissertations that conclude unquestioningly and uncritically that Lewis, an expert marksman and road-hardened explorer, had sloppily committed suicide by shooting himself in the back of the head and chest, and then cutting himself from head to toe with razors. All was done presumably to protect him from enemies that Gilbert and others assert were figments of Lewis's deranged imagination. Lewis was buried hastily along with details of his death and the definitive truth of his killer.

In 1848, nearly forty years after Lewis's demise, the state of Tennessee began an effort to erect a monument at his gravesite. His remains were located, verified, and then reburied. A monument was erected at the site to honor Lewis and his contributions. The monument was made of rough-cut stone at the base, topped with a 12-foot column of Tennessee marble, deliberately broken at the top. The committee report states, "The design is simple, but it is intended to express the difficulties, successes and violent termination of a life which was marked by bold enterprise, by manly courage and devoted patriotism."

What's far more intriguing, however, is the unsolicited questioning of reports about Lewis's death contained in a "Report of the Lewis Monumental Committee," presented to the legislature of 1849–50. It reads, "The impression has long prevailed that under the influence of disease of body and mind—of hopes based upon long and valuable services—not merely deferred, but wholly disappointed—Governor Lewis perished by his own hands," the report reads. "It seems to be more probable that he died by the hands of an assassin."[8]

Tennessee lawyer James D. Park devoted a great deal of time to investigating the cold case of the death of Lewis and delivered his finding in a September 1891 issue of the *Nashville American,* echoing the sentiment expressed in the report by the Lewis Monumental Committee. Park claimed, in what amounted to a legal brief arguing that Lewis was murdered, that no one in the vicinity of Lewis's murder was ever convinced that Lewis committed suicide. He wrote, "It has always been the firm belief of the people of this region that Governor Lewis was murdered and robbed. The oldest citizens now living remember the rumor current at the time as to the murder, and it seems no thought of suicide ever obtained footing here."[9]

Based on interviews with people who were employed at Grinder's

Stand, Park surmised that Lewis had been murdered and robbed by Mr. Grinder. Reports from the region indicated that Grinder had even stood trial for the murder but was acquitted for lack of evidence.

Park, like Coues and others, suggests that Lewis's character, health, and overall mental state at the time of his death stand in contradiction to claims that he committed suicide. Park writes:

> It seems incredible that a young man of 35, the governor of the vast territory of Louisiana, then on his way from the capital to that of his nation, where he knew he would be received with all the distinction and consideration due to his office and reputation, should take his own life. His whole character is a denial of the theory. He was too brave and conscientious in the discharge of every public duty, public and private; too conspicuous a person in the eyes of the country, and crowned with too many laurels, to cowardly sneak out of the world by the back way, a self-murderer. This idea was doubtless invented to cover up the double crime of robbery and murder, and seems to have been the only version of his death that reached Mr. Jefferson and his other friends in Virginia.[10]

The question then remains, who killed Lewis?

One of the most popular and widely accepted murder theories suggests that bandits murdered Lewis during a robbery. The Natchez Trace was a long and treacherous stretch of road through dark woodland, and there were plenty of murders and robberies reported along the trail. But bandits are not the only suspected culprits. Nearly everyone close to Lewis on that fateful night has been listed among potential murder suspects, including Mr. and Mrs. Grinder, Lewis's servant, John Pernier, Major Neelly, a local renegade named Runion, and several native chiefs who reportedly had been traveling with Lewis and Neelly.

Seventy years later journalist and historian Vardis Fisher explored several murder theories in his book *Suicide or Murder? The Strange Death of Governor Meriwether Lewis.* Fisher clearly supports the theory that Lewis was murdered, possibly by conspirators who believed Lewis had a map to a gold mine somewhere in the West.

Historian, journalist, and researcher David Leon Chandler provides an exhaustive explanation of his theory that Lewis was murdered as part of an assassination conspiracy spawned by his old friend Thomas Jefferson. *The Jefferson Conspiracies: A President's Role in the Assassination of Meriwether Lewis* suggests that Lewis discovered certain secrets about General James Wilkinson, his predecessor as governor of Upper Louisiana. If revealed, Chandler surmised, the secrets would destroy the reputations of both General Wilkerson and Jefferson. Chandler speculates that Lewis was not just traveling to Washington to reclaim debts and smooth ruffled feathers. He claims Lewis was traveling to Washington to blow the whistle on Wilkinson and Jefferson. Chandler suggests plausibly that Neelly and Major Russell were also involved in the assassination.[11]

Perhaps the most complete and compelling murder theory comes from James E. Starrs, professor of forensic science at George Washington University, and independent historian Kira Gale. According to Gale's book, *The Death of Meriwether Lewis: A Historic Crime Scene Investigation,* Lewis was likely assassinated by agents sent by then General James Wilkinson and Aaron Burr.

Burr and Lewis had worked together during Jefferson's first administration when Burr was vice president and Lewis worked as Jefferson's private secretary. Lewis was traveling up the Missouri River on the day Burr killed Alexander Hamilton in the now famous duel. After the duel Burr's political career came to a halt. Burr and Wilkinson, meanwhile, began planning to invade Spanish territory with a so-called filibustering expedition. They would lead a private, armed expedition of more than a thousand men into Mexico with the intent of establishing a new government and appointing themselves its leaders.

When Lewis and Clark returned from their expedition west, Burr's plan to invade Mexico overshadowed the triumph of the Corps of Discovery. Burr's invasion was to launch from the private island estate of wealthy Irish aristocrat Harman Blennerhassett, who was said to be funding the expedition. On November 27, 1806, Jefferson ordered the arrest of Burr and his followers on the charge of illegally planning an armed attack on Spanish territory. Two weeks later Blennerhassett and members of the filibuster fled from local militia, who burned Blennerhassett's mansion. The group later met with Burr at the mouth of the Cumberland River in Kentucky.

Meanwhile General Wilkinson, who had been removed from political office as the governor of Upper Louisiana by Jefferson and replaced by Lewis, managed to negotiate peace with Spanish troops that had crossed the Sabine River into the United States. This peace contradicted plans agreed to by Burr and Wilkinson, who were planning to use the Spanish invasion as an excuse to launch their armed invasion of Mexico. Wilkinson, who had been receiving payments for information he had been feeding to the Spanish government, had apparently switched sides. Wilkinson managed to avoid a war with Spain by making a private deal with Spanish General Simon Herrera, who agreed to withdraw his troops. The condition was the creation of a sort of neutral zone on the blurred border between Mexico and the United States. According to Gale, Wilkinson "thus managed to please both his Spanish paymasters and the President, while sacrificing his friend and fellow conspirator, Aaron Burr."[12]

In a message to Congress dated January 12, 1807, Jefferson explained what he described as a plot to separate the western states from the American Union and to invade Mexico. Two days later he held a presidential banquet celebrating the return of Lewis and Clark. Burr, meanwhile, had been arrested at Bayou Pierre near Natchez, Mississippi. Very few people believed at the time that he had planned to separate from the Union, or that he planned to invade Mexico. On February 4, 1807, a grand jury refused to even indict him. Burr then fled, only to be captured a week later and brought to Richmond, Virginia, where he stood trial for treason.

Burr was later acquitted. Wilkinson, in turn, narrowly escaped indictment for treason by a seven-to-nine vote of the grand jury, according to *The Burr Conspiracy* by Thomas Abernathy. During this time the territory that Lewis was to inherit was becoming a political hotbed, as wealthy landowners went to war over vast stores of the lead that had been discovered in the Louisiana Territory. Facing war on several fronts, Congress voted to capitalize and control all land bearing lead throughout the territory. William Carr, federal land agent, remarked that profits from the leasing and sale of public lands would likely be able to pay the $15 million cost of the Louisiana Purchase within a few years. Lands rife with lead became small war zones with armed land speculators battling for control. Most notorious and powerful among them was John Smith T., a relative of General James Wilkinson.

When Lewis was appointed governor of Louisiana Territory he set about "cleaning up" the territory, starting with routing anyone and everyone involved with Aaron Burr. In a letter to William Clark he wrote, "It is my wish that every person who holds an appointment of profit or honor in that territory and against whom sufficient proof of the infection of Burrism can be adduced, should be immediately dismissed from office without partiality favor or affection, as I can never make any terms with traitors."[13]

Lewis's efforts to clean up Louisiana Territory were blocked perpetually by his nemesis Frederick Bates. When Lewis was reported dead Bates expressed little regret. A letter from Bates to James Howe at the time stated bluntly that he "had no personal regard for him and a great deal of political contempt."[14]

In fact, before Lewis was murdered Bates was charged with terrorizing Lewis to the brink of madness. At the time one of Bates' colleagues, Clement Penrose, reported to his brother "that the mental derangement of the Governor ought not to be imputed to his political miscarriages; but rather to the barbarous conduct of the Secretary (Bates). That Mr. Bates determined to tear down Gov. Lewis, at all events, with the hope of supplanting him in the Executive Office with a great deal of scandal equally false and malicious."[15]

A letter to Bates from his sister Nancy bears the alarming statement, "I lament his death on your account, thinking it might involve you in difficulty." The statement suggests that Bates may have been involved in the murder.[16]

Author Jonathan Daniels suggests that Bates was the only one with an immediate and credible motive for wanting Lewis dead. He speculated that Bates "may have been fearful of Wilkinson, with whom he had been 'on very intimate terms,' about something the general required him to keep hidden."[17]

Moreover, Daniels speculates that Wilkinson may very well have helped place the "politically shifting" Bates in his position in St. Louis, hoping that Bates would help cover up his traitorous dealings there. Perhaps, he suggests, Lewis learned something that Bates, Wilkinson, and perhaps even Jefferson wanted to keep secret.

But there are other, equally plausible suspects, including John Smith T.

When Lewis took over his role as Louisiana governor he targeted three men that he considered chief conspirators and impediments to his governing of the territory. The first was John Smith T., who had set off to join Burr in his planned invasion of Mexico until it was discovered that Burr had been routed as a traitor. John Smith T., who added to his name a *T* for "Tennessee," was considered the most dangerous man in Missouri and was known to have murdered more than a dozen men. By the 1820s he was known as the Lead King of Missouri.

Smith T. had brought under his control hundreds of thousands of acres in Tennessee and northern Alabama. Historical accounts suggest that Smith T. handled his affairs with litigation, guns, and hired gunmen. Two of Smith T.'s slaves had become renowned gunsmiths, and he managed a shot tower along the Mississippi River that churned out bullets. Smith T. was ready and frequently willing to supply weapons and ammunition for unauthorized invasions of Mexico. In fact he is known to have participated in at least four attempts to invade Texas and Mexico. When James Wilkinson became the first governor of Louisiana

Territory in 1805–06, he ousted Moses Austin from several key positions and replaced him with Smith T.

In *The Death of Meriwether Lewis,* Gales suggests that a biography of Smith T. by Richard Steward offers a plausible motive for an assassination attempt on Lewis.

> A month before Lewis left St. Louis, a "citizen's committee" in St. Louis chose John Smith T. as a lobbyist to go to Washington, and to bring two petitions to Congress. The first petition asked for the removal from office of Judge John B. C. Lucas, a friend of both Meriwether Lewis and Albert Gallatin, the Secretary of the Treasury. Lucas was one of three land claims commissioners in St. Louis and a Judge of the Territorial Court. As a member of the commission reviewing Spanish land claims, he was blamed for too strictly following the law. In addition, the petitioners wanted the law changed, validating land claims that were recorded after France's secret acquisition of the territory on October 1, 1800.
>
> The second petition asked for a change of status for Louisiana Territory; an upgrade which would allow residents to elect their own territorial officials, rather than be wards of the Federal Government. It was obviously also the intention of the petition leaders to urge that Lewis not be reappointed as Territorial Governor by the President.[18]

Meanwhile Smith T.'s brother Reuben Smith was preparing to make another armed excursion into Mexico. The group was captured by Spanish militia and sent to labor in the mines. Gale notes that Smith T.'s trip to Washington, and his whereabouts at the time, remain a mystery. Gale suggests that Smith T.'s attempts to free Louisiana from federal oversight, the subsequent unauthorized invasion attempt by his brother, the concurring trip by Lewis to Washington to rout so-called Burrites such as Smith T., his brother Reuben, and General James Wilkinson coincide perfectly. Her conclusion is that Lewis was killed by Smith T., or his agents. The motive was to remove Lewis from power so Smith T. and the remaining Burrites could continue to use Louisiana as a staging area for the quest to invade Mexico.

Whether ordered by Wilkinson, Bates, Jefferson, or some other political rival, Lewis had to be removed. His determination, once his mind was set on an objective, knew no way of turning back. This was as true of his desire to fulfill the mandate of his trip with Clark as it was of his intention to clear the Louisiana Territory of corrupt factions of treasonous remnants of Wilkinson's bunch.

Captain Gilbert Russell, during Lewis's last days, wrote that he had planned to travel with the governor to Washington. He had requested a leave of absence from General James Wilkinson but did not receive it when expected. Seemingly frustrated and impatient, Lewis left with Neelly, a friend of Wilkinson, who had appointed Neelly to his position as agent to the Chickasaw Nation. Gale suggests that Neelly had mysteriously arrived at Fort Pickering without explanation and had waited patiently and without reason to travel to Washington with Lewis.

Surrounded on all sides by agents and affiliates of his enemies—Wilkinson, Burr, and Smith T.—Lewis never made it to Washington, D.C.

Afterword

With the unknown, one is confronted with danger, discomfort and worry; the first instinct is to abolish these painful sensations. First principle: any explanation is better than none. The question "Why?" is not pursued for its own sake but to find a certain kind of answer—an answer that is pacifying, tranquilizing and soothing.
FRIEDRICH NIETZSCHE, TWILIGHT OF THE IDOLS

Welcome to the wilderness. Readers expecting a neatly packaged conclusion may be disappointed. But history is complex, messy, sometimes terrifying. Often it's mysterious.

There are a thousand conclusions to draw from what you've just finished reading. But there are far more questions. These are questions that deserve to be asked, even if a convenient answer doesn't immediately present itself.

Was Meriwether Lewis murdered because his journals contained secrets that others wanted to suppress? Did he discover evidence of advanced cultures that might have undermined the moral foundation of planned westward expansion? Or was he murdered because he was in the way of Wilkinson and Smith T. and their nefarious ambitions? Perhaps Lewis, a Master Mason, staunch advocate of state's rights, and an indefatigable hero, became a liability amid political turmoil that ensconced him upon returning from the wilderness. Perhaps Jefferson learned to regret sending Lewis to rout corruption in Louisiana. Did his headstrong friend and former secretary harbor some damning revelations about Jefferson's relationship to Wilkinson and Burr?

The common answers to these kinds of questions often reek of a kind of desperate certainty that belongs more in church than it does in science and academia. Indeed many historians, anthropologists, ethnologists, and other official spokespersons for the dead would like you to believe their version of the past. Many lay claim to history and the truth like greedy land speculators. But, to quote Nietzsche again, we are all better artists than we realize. If you need evidence, take the time to look at the amazing variety of theories and conclusions drawn about the smallest portion of American history. Then recognize that no matter how contradictory, each one is presented with incredible conviction.

History is as much a work of art as it is a science. Personal preference; the rush to certainty; the need to trump rival theories or rival professors; the need for a comfortable conclusion; the desire to contribute something novel enough to the conversation to earn tenure—all these are as real and present as the motivation to seek and codify the truth.

We construct history from evidence, sure. But there's more to it.

Meriwether Lewis explored the wilderness. Ultimately he paid a price for it. When there are resources to be plundered, the truth becomes a liability, an inconvenience. That's true whether the resources are vast stores of lead, gold, timber, and land, or the resources produced by the publishing of a book. We lay no claim to the truth. Like Lewis, we're comfortable in the wilderness.

But there remains a hunger for the so-called truth. Even when a thousand meticulously researched theories have been constructed and presented, people continue to question. People know when they've got only part of the story. But often the need for resolution, notoriety, control, or a quick buck overwhelms the need for truth. That's true regardless of the source. Whether it's the sanctioned proclamations of a university professor or the desperate ranting of the latest conspiracy researcher, most of us know deep down when someone is offering speculation disguised as truth.

But this is more than an intellectual exercise. There are a hundred members of Meriwether Lewis's family who want to know if he was murdered. It's been more than a decade since James Starrs filed an affidavit to convene a coroner's jury in the Tennessee County where Lewis was killed. During the summer of 1996, in Hohenwald, Tennessee, a group gathered to hear testimony from historians, forensic scientists, and experts who offered their opinions on the value of exhuming Lewis's body. The participants, nearly all of whom said they believed Lewis was murdered, recommended that his remains be exhumed with hope that modern forensic techniques would help solve the mystery of his death. The National Park Service has consistently stood in the way of requests to do so. The Park Service says that participants in the jury offered a one-sided view of Lewis's death. Officials suggested that the sanctity of the monument was more important than the promise of new information contained in a body that has been decaying for two centuries.

Robert C. Haraden, former superintendent of the Natchez Trace Parkway & Meriwether Lewis National Monument, wrote:

> There are people who believe that Lewis committed suicide and others who believe he was murdered. Both groups are well intentioned. However, the mystery, the fascination, and the lore of Lewis and Clark and their heroic expedition is that we do not know every detail about them. Nor do we need to know—that's what keeps the story alive. . . . There is a high potential for damage to the monument and gravesite [from exhumation] and only a forlorn hope that anything positive can be learned after 190 years. . . . Let's not dwell on Meriwether Lewis' death. Instead, let us celebrate his life and great accomplishments and let the mystery remain.[1]

Or maybe, just maybe, going just a bit deeper into the wilderness would serve another purpose. Maybe learning the truth about Lewis's demise would help hundreds, perhaps thousands, of people find a peace that has eluded them. Maybe learning the truth would shed new light on the past we thought we knew, thereby changing the present, and the future. Maybe digging for the truth of America's history would violate the territory claimed by the Parks Service, the Smithsonian Institution, and the Ivy League. Someone might have to add a footnote to their lecture materials. Someone might have to come up with an extra line item on their annual budget. Someone might have to dig around in the vast stores of antiquities that have been cataloged but never explored or presented as part of history. Someone might have to admit that they didn't get it all right the first time.

More than that, though, someone might have to admit that burying the truth for the sake of celebrating the life of a man who was murdered, cultures that were murdered, or a country that was built on murder, isn't really much of a celebration at all.

Notes

INTRODUCTION

1. Ambrose, *Undaunted Courage,* 76.

CHAPTER 1. THE OLMEC RIDDLES

1. Whittaker, *Africans in the Americas: Our Journey Throughout the World,* 15.
2. O'Halleran, "Another Mystery of Mesoamerica."
3. Hancock, *Fingerprints of the Gods,* 124–25.
4. Ibid., 137.
5. Ibid., 140.
6. Ibid., 148–49.
7. Stengel, "The Diffusionists Have Landed," 35–48.
8. Diehl, *The Olmecs: America's First Civilization.*
9. *Science Daily.* "Researchers Find Evidence of the Earliest Writing in the New World."
10. Cooper, *Leap of Faith,* 211.
11. Ibid., 214.

CHAPTER 2. FLORIDA AND THE FOUNTAIN OF YOUTH

1. Cabeza de Vaca, *Spanish Explorers in the Southern United States,* 31–32; Bourne, *A Narrative of de Soto's Expedition.*
2. Lasater, *Spain to England;* Reuters, "Copperfield 'Finds Fountain of Youth.'"

CHAPTER 3. THE MYSTERIES OF THE MISSISSIPPI MOUND BUILDERS

1. Bourne, *Narratives of the Career of Hernando De Soto.*
2. Silverberg, *The Mound Builders,* 259–64.
3. Hamilton, "A Tradition of Giants and Ancient American Warfare," 6–13.
4. Gauss, *We the People,* 297.
5. To John C. Breckenridge, Monticello, August 12, quoted in DeConde, *This Affair of Louisiana,* 183–84.
6. Baker, *From Savage to Negro,* 26–54.
7. Powell, *From Barbarism to Civilization,* 109.
8. Mann, *1491,* 4.
9. Ibid.
10. Ibid., 9.
11. Ibid.
12. Ibid., 13.
13. Ibid.
14. Hamilton, *The Mystery of the Serpent Mound.*
15. Lewis and Ordway, *The Journals of Captain Meriwether Lewis and Seargeant John Ordway,* 40.
16. Lewis and Clark, *The Definitive Journals of Lewis & Clark, Vol. 2,* 505.
17. Saindon, "Lewis and Clark and the Legend of the 'Little People,'" 478.
18. Romain, "Serpent Mound Revisited."

CHAPTER 4. LEWIS AND CLARK AND THE JOURNEY WEST

1. Lewis and Clark, *The Definitive Journals of Lewis & Clark, Vol. 9,* 233.
2. Ibid., 234.
3. Allen, "Cahokia Mounds Finding Stuns Archaeologists."
4. Ibid.
5. Moulton, "The Missing Journals of Meriwether Lewis," 28–39.

CHAPTER 5. PRINCE MADOC, WELSH NATIVES, AND LEGENDS OF THE MANDAN

1. Lewis and Clark, *The Lewis and Clark Journals,* 241.
2. Lewis and Clark, *The Definitive Journals of Lewis and Clark, Vol. 8,* xv.
3. Powel, *The Historie of Cambria,* 166–67.

4. Lewis and Clark, *The Lewis and Clark Journals*, 442.

5. Donnelly, *Atlantis*, 115.

6. Catlin, *Illustrations of the Manners, Customs, and Condition of the North American Indian*, 93.

7. Ibid., 93.

8. Ibid., 259.

9. Donnelly, *Atlantis*, 111.

10. Ibid., 98.

11. Catlin, *Illustrations of the Manners, Customs, and Condition of the American Indian*, 182.

CHAPTER 6. VOYAGERS OF THE PACIFIC COAST AND THE KENNEWICK MAN

1. Ambrose, *Undaunted Courage*, 484; Slaughter, *Exploring Lewis and Clark*, 153.

2. Lewis and Clark, *The Definitive Journals of Lewis and Clark, Vol. 5*, 211.

3. Lewis and Clark, *The Lewis and Clark Journals*, 246.

4. Lewis and Clark, *The Definitive Journals of Lewis and Clark, Vol. 5*, 328.

5. Chief Joseph of the Niimiipu Nation, *Great Speeches by Native Americans*, 150.

6. Lewis and Clark, *The Definitive Journals of Lewis and Clark, Vol. 5*, 328.

7. King, "Kennewick Man's Bones Provide Window to Past."

8. Strang, "Kennewick Man's Secrets Still Mostly Secret."

9. Ibid.

10. Cremo and Thompson, *The Hidden History of the Human Race*, 90.

11. Stiger, *Worlds Before Our Own*.

12. Dubois, "On A Quasi Coin Reported Found in a Boring in Illinois," 224.

13. Cremo and Thompson, *The Hidden History of the Human Race*, 802.

14. Peet, *Underground!*, 320.

CHAPTER 7. GIANTS IN ANCIENT AMERICA

1. Oberlander, "Has the Biblical Goliath Been Found?"

2. Durán, *The Aztecs: The History of the Indies of New Spain*.

3. Díaz, *The Conquest of New Spain*, 181.

4. Pigafetta and Ashlin Skelton, *Magellan's Voyage*, 46.

5. Vespucci, *The First Four Voyages of Amerigo Vespucci*, 30.

6. Pohl, *Amerigo Vespucci*, 85.

7. Keith and Parry, *New Iberian World,* 162.

8. Cody, *An Autobiography of Buffalo Bill,* 197.

9. Ibid., 197.

10. O'Farrell, "Diver 'Vanishes' in Portal to Maya Underworld."

CHAPTER 8. THE HERO RETURNS

1. Lewis and Clark, *The Definitive Journals of Lewis and Clark, Vol. 8,* 134.

2. Fleming, "Stone Secrets of the First Americans."

CHAPTER 9. FRIENDS IN HIGH PLACES

1. Washington, *The Writings of George Washington,* vol. 14, 119.

2. Willard, *A Sermon Preached in Lancaster,* 14–15.

3. Hodgson Brown and Simpson, *Web of Debt,* 75.

4. Waltzek, *Wealth Building Strategies in Energy, Metals and Other Markets,* 176.

5. Moulton, "The Missing Journals of Meriwether Lewis," 28.

6. Ibid., 29.

7. Ibid.

CHAPTER 10. THE MURDER OF MERIWETHER LEWIS

1. Jefferson, *The Writings of Thomas Jefferson, Vol. 5,* 320.

2. Guice and Buckley, *The Mysterious Death of Meriwether Lewis,* 32.

3. Chuinard, "How Did Meriwether Lewis Die?," 1222.

4. Gale, "Was Clark Deceived About Lewis's Suicide?"

5. Coues, *History of the Expedition Under the Command of Captains Lewis and Clark,* xliv–xlvi.

6. Ibid., xliii–xlvi.

7. Ibid., xxxix.

8. Ibid., lxi.

9. Ibid., liii.

10. Ibid., lv.

11. Chandler, *The Jefferson Conspiracies.*

12. Gale, "Aaron Burr, Meriwether Lewis and the Burr-Wilkinson Conspiracy, Part 2."

13. Gale, "Were Lead Mines the Reason Meriwether Lewis Was Murdered?"

14. Saindon, "Lewis and Clark and the Legend of the 'Little People,'" 1188.

15. Daniels, *The Devil's Backbone*, 186.

16. Ibid., 187.

17. Ibid., 188.

18. Gale and Starrs, *The Death of Meriwether Lewis.*

AFTERWORD

1. Haraden, "Letter to the Editor," 3.

Bibliography

Allen, William. "Cahokia Mounds Finding Stuns Archaeologists: A Large Stone Under the Site's Biggest Mound May Be a Man-Made Structure." *St. Louis Post-Dispatch*, March 9, 1998.

Ambrose, Stephen. *Undaunted Courage: Meriwether Lewis, Thomas Jefferson, and the Opening of the American West*. New York: Simon & Schuster, 1997.

Baker, Lee D. *From Savage to Negro: Anthropology and the Construction of Race, 1896–1954*. Berkeley: University of California Press, 1998.

Bourne, Edward Gaylord. *A Narrative of de Soto's Expedition Based on the Diary of Rodrigo Ranjel, His Private Secretary in 1546*. New York: Allerton Book Company, 1904.

———. *Narratives of the Career of Hernando De Soto in the Conquest of Florida: As Told by a Knight of Elvas, and in a Relation by Luys Hernández De Biedma, Factor of the Expedition*, vol. 2. Toronto: Nabu Press, 2010.

Brown, Ellen Hodgson, and Reed Simpson. *Web of Debt: The Shocking Truth About Our Money System and How We Can Break Free*. Baton Rouge, La.: Third Millennium Press, 2008.

Cabeza de Vaca, Alvar Nunez. *Spanish Explorers in the Southern United States*. New York: Barnes & Noble, 1959.

Catlin, George. *Illustrations of the Manners, Customs, and Condition of the North American Indian*, vol. 1. London: Henry G. Bohn, 1866.

Chandler, David Leon. *The Jefferson Conspiracies: A President's Role in the Assassination of Meriwether Lewis*. New York: Morrow, 1994.

Chief Joseph, et al. *Great Speeches by Native Americans.* Edited by Bob Blaisdell. Mineola, N.Y.: Dover Publications Inc., 2000.

Chuinard, E. G. "How Did Meriwether Lewis Die? It Was Murder." *Explorations into the World of Lewis and Clark: Essays from the Pages of We Proceeded On, the Quarterly Journal of the Lewis and Clark Trail Heritage Foundation.* Scituate, Mass.: Digital Scanning, 2003.

Cody, William Frederick. *An Autobiography of Buffalo Bill.* New York: General Books, 2010.

Cooper, Gordon. *Leap of Faith: An Astronaut's Journey into the Unknown.* New York: HarperTorch, 2002.

Coues, Elliot. *History of the Expedition Under the Command of Captains Lewis and Clark,* vol. 1. New York: Dover, 1893.

Cremo, Michael, and Richard Thompson. *The Hidden History of the Human Race,* abridged ed. San Bruno, Calif.: Audio Literature, 1997.

Daniels, Jonathan. *The Devil's Backbone: The Story of the Natchez Trace.* New York: McGraw Hill, 1962.

DeConde, Alexander. *This Affair of Louisiana.* New York: Scribner, 1976.

Díaz, Bernal. *The Conquest of New Spain.* London: Penguin, 1967.

Diehl, Richard A. *The Olmecs: America's First Civilization.* New York: Thames & Hudson, 2005.

Donnelly, Ignatius. *Atlantis: The Antedilivuan World.* New York: General Books, 2010.

Dubois, W. E. "On A Quasi Coin Reported Found in a Boring in Illinois." Proceedings of the American Philosophical Society, vol. XII. Philadelphia: M'Calla and Stavely, 1878.

Durán, Diego. *The Aztecs: The History of the Indies of New Spain.* Auckland, New Zealand: Orion Press, 1964.

Fleming, Thomas. "Stone Secrets of the First Americans." The Ensign Message: Official Journal of the Ensign Trust. www.ensignmessage.com/archives/stonesecrets.html (accessed January 8, 2009).

Gale, Kira. "Aaron Burr, Meriwether Lewis and the Burr-Wilkinson Conspiracy, Part 2." Lewis and Clark Travel. www.lewisandclarktravel.com (accessed November 8, 2010).

———. "Was Clark Deceived About Lewis's Suicide?" Lewis and Clark Travel. www.lewisandclarktravel.com (accessed November 8, 2010).

———. "Were Lead Mines the Reason Meriwether Lewis Was Murdered?" Lewis and Clark Travel. www.lewisandclarktravel.com (accessed November 8, 2010).

Gale, Kira, and James E. Starrs. *The Death of Meriwether Lewis: A Historic Crime Scene Investigation.* Omaha, Neb.: River Junction Press, 2009.

Gauss, James. *We the People: Volume II Birth of a Nation.* Bloomington, Ind.: Authorhouse, 2005.

Guice, John D. W., and Jay H. Buckley. *The Mysterious Death of Meriwether Lewis.* Norman, Okla.: University of Oklahoma Press, 2006.

Hamilton, Ross. *The Mystery of the Serpent Mound: In Search of the Alphabet Gods.* Berkeley, Calif.: Frog Ltd, 2001.

———. "A Tradition of Giants and Ancient American Warfare." *Ancient American* (Spring 2001).

Hancock, Graham. *Fingerprints of the Gods.* New York: Three Rivers Press, 1996.

Haraden, Robert C. "Letter to the Editor." *We Proceeded On,* (February 2002).

Jefferson, Thomas. *The Writings of Thomas Jefferson,* vol. 5. New York: Riker, Thorne, 1854.

Keith, Robert G., and J. H. Parry. *New Iberian World: A Documentary History of the Discovery and Settlement of Latin America to the Early 17th Century,* vol. 1. Sacramento, Calif.: Garland Science, 1988.

King, Anna. "Kennewick Man's Bones Provide Window to Past." *Tri-City Herald.* Kennewick, August 30, 2002.

Lasater, Alice E. *Spain to England: A Comparative Study of Arabic, European, and English Literature of the Middle Ages.* Jackson, Mich.: University Press of Mississippi, 1974.

Lewis, Meriwether, and William Clark. *The Definitive Journals of Lewis & Clark, Vol. 2: From the Ohio to the Vermillion.* Edited by Gary E. Moulton. Lincoln, Neb.: University of Nebraska Press, 1986.

———. *The Definitive Journals of Lewis and Clark, Vol. 5: Through the Rockies to the Cascades.* Edited by Gary E. Moulton. Lincoln, Neb.: University of Nebraska Press, 1988.

———. *The Definitive Journals of Lewis and Clark, Vol. 8: Over the Rockies to St. Louis.* Edited by Gary E. Moulton. Toronto: Bison Books, 2002.

———. *The Definitive Journals of Lewis & Clark, Vol. 9: The Journals of John Ordway, May 14, 1804–September 23, 1806 and Charles Floyd, May 14–August 18.* Edited by Gary E. Moulton. Lincoln, Neb.: University of Nebraska Press, 1986.

———. *The Lewis and Clark Journals (Abridged Edition): An American Epic of Discovery,* 2nd ed. Edited by Gary E. Moulton. Toronto: Bison Books, 2003.

Lewis, Meriwether, and John Ordway. *The Journals of Captain Meriwether Lewis and Seargeant John Ordway: Kept on the Expedition of Western Exploration, 1803–1806.* Edited by Milo M. Quaife. Madison, Wis.: State Historical Society of Wisconsin, 1916.

Mann, Charles C. *1491: New Revelations of the Americas Before Columbus.* New York: Vintage Books/Random House, 2006.

Moulton, Gary E. "The Missing Journals of Meriwether Lewis." *Montana: The Magazine of Western History* 35, Summer 1985.

Oberlander, Elana. "Has the Biblical Goliath Been Found?" IMRA—Middle East News and Analysis (November 10, 2005). www.imra.org.il (accessed November 8, 2010).

O'Farrell, Marty. "Diver 'Vanishes' in Portal to Maya Underworld." *National Geographic Daily News,* June 29, 2010.

O'Halleran, Kathy. "Another Mystery of Mesoamerica: The Enigma of the Olmecs." Suite101.com (September 4, 1999). www.suite101.com/article.cfm/history_mesoamerica_retired/25177/2.

Peet, Preston. *Underground! The Disinformation Guide to Ancient Civilizations.* New York: The Disinformation Company, 2005.

Pigafetta, Antonio, and Raleigh Ashlin Skelton. *Magellan's Voyage: A Narrative Account of the First Circumnavigation.* New York: Dover, 1994.

Pohl, Frederick Julius. *Amerigo Vespucci: Pilot Major.* New York: Octagon Books, 1996.

Powel, David. *The Historie of Cambria, Now Called Wales.* London: Reprinted for John Harding, 1584.

Powell, John Wesley. *From Barbarism to Civilization.* Washington, D.C.: American Anthropological Association, 1888.

Reuters. "Copperfield Finds 'Fountain of Youth.'" ABC News Online, August 16, 2006. www.abc.net.

Romain, W. F. "Serpent Mound Revisited." *Ohio Archaeologist* 37, no. 4, 1987.

Saindon, Robert A. "Lewis and Clark and the Legend of the 'Little People.'" *Explorations into the World of Lewis and Clark: Essays from the Pages of We Proceeded On, the Quarterly Journal of the Lewis and Clark Trail Heritage Foundation.* Scituate, Mass.: Digital Scanning, 2003.

Science Daily. "Researchers Find Evidence of the Earliest Writing in the New World" (September 15, 2006). www.sciencedaily.com/releases/2006/09/060914154552.htm (accessed November 8, 2010).

Silverberg, Robert. *The Mound Builders*. Athens, Ohio: Ohio University Press, 1986.

Slaughter, Thomas P. *Exploring Lewis and Clark: Reflections of Men in the Wilderness*. New York: First Vintage Books, 2003.

Stengel, Mark K. "The Diffusionists Have Landed." *The Atlantic Monthly*, January 2000.

Stiger, Brad. *Worlds Before Our Own*. New York: Berkley Books, 1979.

Strang, John. "Kennewick Man's Secrets Still Mostly Secret." *Seattle Post Intelligencer*, July 13, 2009.

Vespucci, Amerigo. *The First Four Voyages of Amerigo Vespucci* (Florence, 1505–6). Toronto: Nabu Press, 2010.

Waltzek, Chris. *Wealth Building Strategies in Energy, Metals and Other Markets*. Hoboken, N.J.: Wiley, 2010.

Washington, George. *The Writings of George Washington*, vol. 14. New York: G. P. Putnam's Sons, 1893.

Whittaker, Sabas H. *Africans in the Americas Our Journey Throughout the World: The Long African Journey Throughout the World Our History A Short Stop in the Americas*. New York: iUniverse, 2003.

Willard, Joseph. *A Sermon Preached in Lancaster . . . on the Anniversary of Our National Independence . . . Before the Washington Benevolent Societies of Lancaster and Guildhall*. Windsor, Vt.: Thomas M. Pomeroy, 1812.

Index

Page numbers in *italics* represent illustrations.

BOOKS OF RELATED INTEREST

The Suppressed History of American Banking
How Big Banks Fought Jackson, Killed Lincoln, and Caused the Civil War
by Xaviant Haze

Aliens in Ancient Egypt
The Brotherhood of the Serpent and the Secrets of the Nile Civilization
by Xaviant Haze

The Secret Life of Lady Liberty
Goddess in the New World
by Robert Hieronimus, Ph.D., and Laura Cortner

Founding Fathers, Secret Societies
Freemasons, Illuminati, Rosicrucians, and the Decoding of the Great Seal
by Robert Hieronimus, Ph.D., with Laura Cortner

The Ancient Giants Who Ruled America
The Missing Skeletons and the Great Smithsonian Cover-Up
by Richard J. Dewhurst

America: Nation of the Goddess
The Venus Families and the Founding of the United States
by Alan Butler and Janet Wolter
Foreword by Scott F. Wolter

Advanced Civilizations of Prehistoric America
The Lost Kingdoms of the Adena, Hopewell, Mississippians, and Anasazi
by Frank Joseph

Lost Race of the Giants
The Mystery of Their Culture, Influence,
and Decline throughout the World
by Patrick Chouinard

Inner Traditions • Bear & Company
P.O. Box 388
Rochester, VT 05767
1-800-246-8648
www.InnerTraditions.com

Or contact your local bookseller